THE CHURCH AND CHRISTIAN EDUCATION

PAUL H. VIETH, *Editor*

Published for the
COOPERATIVE PUBLISHING ASSOCIATION

By
THE BETHANY PRESS
St. Louis

The Scripture quotations in this book are from the Revised Standard Version of the New Testament, copyright, 1946, by the Division of Christian Education of the National Council of the Churches of Christ in the United States of America and are used by permission.

COPYRIGHT, 1947

By

C. D. PANTLE

First Printing, February, 1947

Second Printing, August, 1947

Third Printing, November, 1947

Fourth Printing, October, 1948

Fifth Printing, March, 1949

Sixth Printing, November, 1949

Seventh Printing, July, 1951

Eighth Printing, January, 1953

Printed in the United States of America

To

PERCY ROY HAYWARD

Pioneer in Christian Education
and
Long-Time Staff Member
of the
International Council of Religious Education

Wise in Counsel, Steadfast in Friendship, Brother in Christ

Preface

*T*HE International Council of Religious Education, at its annual meeting in February, 1944, authorized an inquiry into the present status of Christian education and made provision for a committee to undertake it. The action included an expression of a sense of need of "special study and consideration of such problems as the following:

"*a*) Conditions precipitated by the war, taking account of the necessary adjustments in the program of Christian education to meet the needs of the new situation and of men and women returned from military and defense services.*

"*b*) The need of a considered statement as to the place of theological and other concepts in Christian education.

"*c*) The educational opportunity and responsibility presented by the forthcoming publication of the new Revised Standard Version of the English Bible.*

"*d*) The place of the educational program and of the educational method in the total program of the church, the home and the community.

"*e*) The urgent need of new ways of serving the unreached part of the constituency.

"*f*) The need of plans for securing a more adequate lay and professional leadership.

"*g*) The incorporation of the ecumenical Christian ideal in the program of Christian education and the conscious participation of the International Council in the world-wide movement in Christian education.

"*h*) A definition of the functions of the inter-church agency of Christian education and of its committees and other groups.

"*i*) The basic issues involved in accepted organizations and patterns of work."

*These responsibilities were later assigned to other committees of the Council.

At the same meeting the Council appointed an Administrative Committee to nominate the personnel of the Study Committee to the officers of the Council, and "to make plans for the first meeting along such lines as selecting a place and date and collecting various information including the reports of studies already made."

In selecting the personnel of the Committee on the Study of Christian Education, the Administrative Committee took care to include, not only persons who have been active in the religious education movement, but also representative leaders and specialists in other phases of the church's life and work.

The Study Committee met as a whole on four occasions, each time holding three-day sessions. Each of the seven committees into which the group soon divided held additional meetings.

A request was made at the first meeting of the Committee on the Study of Christian Education that the committee "be permitted to issue its findings in the form of a report addressed to the Council, but on the authority and responsibility of the committee." This request was granted by the International Council in February, 1945.

The 1946 annual meeting of the International Council received reports on "The Local Church," "The Family," and "Leadership," together with a Foreword, entitled "Christian Education—Yesterday and Today," all four documents having earlier been reviewed, revised, and approved by the Study Committee. A fifth document was also presented for information, the report of the Committee on "Theological and Educational Foundations," which had not been before the Study Committee.

The 1947 annual meeting of the International Council, to be held in Grand Rapids, Michigan, will receive the final report of the Study Committee, including those reports yet to be presented: "The Curriculum," "The Community Approach," and "The Structure and Functions of Agencies."

The documents which have been prepared for the various aspects of this study and approved by action of the Committee on the Study of Christian Education can be purchased from the Business Department of the International Council of Religious Education, 203 North Wabash Avenue, Chicago 1, Illinois. The present volume has been prepared as a more popular statement of the implications and findings of the study, by request of the Committee on the Study of Christian Education and of the International Council. The chairman of the Committee on the Study has served as editor for this volume. This book stands in a peculiar relationship to the "Study of Christian Education" itself. The assignment was to prepare a volume for general reading, touching the important aspects and problems of Christian education today, as covered by the "Study," but with entire freedom to use the committee's reports, to rewrite these reports where necessary for the purpose of this volume, or to create new material where points seemed to be needed with which the committee had not dealt. The editor cannot, therefore, take the credit for anything good which may be in this book, for it was probably the work of the committee. On the other hand, he cannot shift the blame to the committee for anything which is bad, for it is probably bad because he misinterpreted the committee, or sought to interpret points on which the committee had not spoken. The critical reader is advised to examine the complete reports of the "Study," in addition to reading this book.

THE CHURCH AND CHRISTIAN EDUCATION

The editor and executive secretary express their appreciation to all the members of the committee for their cooperation in this study and their contributions of time and work. In particular, the editor wishes to thank those who read parts of this manuscript and made suggestions on it.

PAUL II. VIETH, *Chairman and Editor*

GERALD E. KNOFF, *Executive Secretary*

September 10, 1946

Members of the Committee on the Study of Christian Education

O. V. Anderson, pastor, Grace Lutheran Church, La Grange, Illinois

Edwin E. Aubrey, president, Crozer Theological Seminary

Frederick H. Bair, professor, University of the State of New York

Isaac K. Beckes, director of young people's work, International Council of Religious Education

John C. Bennett, professor of theology, Union Theological Seminary

C. A. Bowen, executive editor, Editorial Division, Methodist Church

H. R. Bowen, acting general secretary, New Jersey Council of Religious Education

Atha S. Bowman, director of Children's Division, Presbyterian Church, U. S.

Arlo Ayres Brown, president, Drew University

Lin D. Cartwright, editorial secretary, Christian Board of Publication, Disciples of Christ

Morse A. Cartwright, executive secretary, American Association of Adult Education

H. Almond Chaffee, president of City Savings Bank, Bridgeport, Connecticut

W. Norman Cook, Department of Field Program, Presbyterian Church, U. S.

Alvin John Cooper, Department of Young People's Work and Boys' Work, United Church of Canada, Toronto, Canada

Clarence T. Craig, professor, New Testament Department, Oberlin Graduate School of Theology

11

James W. Eichelberger, secretary of Christian education, African Methodist Episcopal Zion Church

Grace Loucks Elliott, general secretary, Young Women's Christian Association

Harrison S. Elliott, professor, Union Theological Seminary

Willis R. Ford, executive secretary, Council of Churches and Christian Education of Maryland-Delaware

Edward D. Grant, executive secretary, Religious Education Committee, Presbyterian Church, U. S.

Frank Grebe, director of religious education, Westminster Church, Buffalo, New York

William Grime, pastor, St. Paul's Episcopal Church, Great Neck, Long Island, New York

Ralph W. Gwinn, congressman, United States Congress, lawyer, New York City

Samuel L. Hamilton, School of Education, New York University

John W. Harms, executive secretary, Church Federation of Greater Chicago

Nevin C. Harner, president, Heidelberg College, Tiffin, Ohio

J. A. Heck, president, Evangelical School of Theology, Reading, Pennsylvania

Seward Hiltner, Commission on Religion and Health, Federal Council of the Churches of Christ in America

Richard Hoiland, secretary, Christian Education Department, Northern Baptist Convention

W. L. Jenkins, general manager, Westminster Press

F. Ernest Johnson, Department of Research and Education, Federal Council of the Churches of Christ in America

MEMBERS OF STUDY COMMITTEE

Mary Alice Jones, children's editor, Rand McNally Publishing Company

Bertha Judd, Commission on Home and Family, Brooklyn Federation of Churches

Paul B. Kern, resident bishop, Nashville Area, Methodist Church

Gerald E. Knoff, associate general secretary, International Council of Religious Education

Paul M. Limbert, president-elect, Springfield Y.M.C.A. College

John L. Lobingier, secretary of religious education, Massachusetts Congregational Conference

John A. Mackay, president, Princeton Theological Seminary

Spencer Miller, Jr., labor specialist

Harry C. Munro, director of educational evangelism, Internationl Council of Religious Education and Federal Council of the Churches of Christ in America

Miles Murphy, professor of psychology, University of Pennsylvania

O. Frederick Nolde, professor of religious education, Mount Airy Lutheran Theological Seminary

G. Bromley Oxnam, resident bishop, New York Area, Methodist Church

Edward B. Paisley, secretary, Division of Education in Home, Church, and Community, Presbyterian Church, U.S.A.

Mark Rich, town and country work, American Baptist Home Mission Society

Roy G. Ross, general secretary, International Council of Religious Education

John W. Rustin, pastor, Mount Vernon Place Methodist Church, Washington, D. C.

John Q. Schisler, executive secretary, Board of Education, Methodist Church

Erwin L. Shaver, director of weekday religious education, International Council of Religious Education

Lewis J. Sherrill, Louisville Presbyterian Theological Seminary

H. Shelton Smith, professor of Christian ethics, Duke University School of Religion

Irving R. Smith, superintendent of the First Baptist Sunday School, Arlington, New Jersey

Harry T. Stock, general secretary, Division of Christian Education, Congregational Christian Churches

Hillyer H. Straton, pastor, First Baptist Church, Malden, Massachusetts

Willis Sutton, Educational Department, *Reader's Digest*

T. T. Swearingen, director of adult work and family education, International Council of Religious Education

Herman J. Sweet, director of leadership education and church school administration, International Council of Religious Education

Paul H. Vieth, professor of Christian nurture, Yale Divinity School

Gertrude L. Warren, director of 4-H Club work, United States Department of Agriculture

Theodore O. Wedel, College of Preachers, Washington, D. C.

Luther A. Weigle, dean, Yale Divinity School

In addition, the following persons were coopted for the special work of some of the committees:

Everett Babcock, executive secretary, Ohio Conference, Congregational Christian Churches

Rex S. Clements, pastor, Bryn Mawr Presbyterian Church, Bryn Mawr, Pennsylvania

Wayne K. Clymer, professor, Evangelical Theological Seminary, Naperville, Illinois.

Cameron P. Hall, Department of Social Relations, Federal Council of the Churches of Christ in America

William Ralph Hall, secretary, Division of Field Service, Presbyterian Church, U. S. A.

Ray J. Harmelink, assistant to general secretary, Presbyterian Church, U. S. A.

Philip C. Landers, associate general secretary, International Council of Religious Education

C. A. Myers, secretary, Board of Christian Education, United Church of Canada

A. N. Sayres, professor, Evangelical and Reformed Seminary, Lancaster, Pennsylvania

Oscar J. Rumpf, director of adult work, Evangelical and Reformed Church

D. M. Shonting, Wartburg Press, American Lutheran Church

Fred D. Stone, publishing agent, Methodist Publishing House

Contents

Chapter I

Christian Education—Yesterday and Today

CHRISTIAN education is as old as Christianity itself. It is a characteristic tendency of man to seek to extend his most cherished beliefs and acts to others. He teaches them to his children. He seeks to convert his fellow men. Even if he did not consciously teach his beliefs, he would still pass them on to those who are most closely associated with him by the influence which comes through living together.

The church has always shown zeal for nurturing its children in the faith as well as for winning adult converts. This concern is seen in the catechetical instruction of the ancient church, in books and treatises, in liturgy and sermons. It appears again in the cathedral and monastic schools of the Middle Ages. With the Reformation there came a new interest in and need for Christian education for all the people. Once again we see an emphasis on the teaching of the Bible and the catechism. The Sunday school advanced rapidly in popularity and influence. Always in Christian families there have been devout expressions of the Christian faith and life which have profoundly influenced young and old.

Yet Christian education as we know it today is distinctly a modern development. Its institutional forms are creatures of comparatively recent years.

Only a hundred years have elapsed since Horace Bushnell published his epoch-making book, *Christian Nurture*. His basic proposition "that the child is to grow up a Christian, and never know himself as being otherwise" is now widely known and accepted. While Horace Bushnell developed his thesis almost exclusively in reference to Christian nurture in the family, he has profoundly influenced the development of agencies for Christian education within the church. Indeed, it is only recently that the significance of the family in any plan for Christian education has been seriously taken into account by the modern Christian education movement.

Education in America in its beginning was basically Christian in motive and content. With the passing of the years two tendencies have developed in public education. One is the extension of education to include more and more people and to embrace more and more completely the areas of human interest and living, rather than limiting itself to fundamental processes of human communication such as reading and writing. The other is to exclude religion from its curriculum, on the ground that it cannot properly be dealt with in a common school which includes all the children of Jews, Catholics, and Protestants with their many divisions, as well as the children of unbelievers.

The first of these tendencies has made it imperative for the church to be zealous in the extension of Christian education. The second has laid upon the churches the obligation to provide Christian education for the children of Christian parents, and at least some form of religious education for all. It is widely assumed that education without religion is not fair either to religion or the children, or the future of the state itself. It is accepted by almost all churches that Christian education is basic to their purpose and work.

In the discharge of these obligations the Protestant churches have developed an extensive program of Christian education. This total program includes such separate strands as the Sunday school, the young people's society, the vacation church school, the weekday church school, the summer conference, and Christian literature. But there is a growing feeling that no one of these, or all of them taken together, constitutes an adequate program. It is the church itself which must be the chief Christian educator, and these separate agencies will achieve their ends only to the extent that they are part and parcel of the whole church in its faith and life.

How effectively the Protestant Christian churches are discharging their obligation to provide Christian education for all those not embraced in the membership of other religious groups is the purpose of this study to discover.

I. THE SUNDAY SCHOOL

Our story of the development of Christian education properly begins with the Sunday school. It was the first of the church's present agencies for Christian education to get under way. It has succeeded in maintaining itself at the center of the church's educational program through the years.

While there were earlier attempts to teach religion on Sunday in conjunction with the regular services of the church, the date for the origin of the Sunday school is usually fixed at 1780. In that year the greathearted Christian layman, Robert Raikes, printer and publisher by trade, had impressed upon him the sad condition of the children of his native city, Gloucester, England.

They were ragged, dirty, profane, delinquent, under-privileged, ignorant. After experimenting with other ways of bettering their condition, he decided on the method of education. So in 1780 he gathered some of them together on Sunday, because it was the only day of the week when they were free from work. The primary purpose of the school was to give these children the rudiments of education, but this did not exclude religion. The venture began with four paid teachers and a five-hour session—from ten to twelve in the morning and from one to four in the afternoon.

Despite determined opposition from various quarters, the venture was successful and grew rapidly. Within five years it had reached the central metropolis of the land, and the Sunday School Society of London was organized. In the same year, 1785, the first Sunday school in the United States of which we have certain knowledge was instituted. Five years later a society for the promotion of the Sunday school was organized in Philadelphia, known as the First Day or Sunday School Society. The new agency was seized upon by the Wesleyan revival and made into a powerful evangelistic tool. In 1825 the American Sunday School Union was established, and its missionaries carried the new institution to the American frontier with zeal and evangelistic passion. Beginning in 1832, conventions of Sunday school workers were periodically held, resulting eventually in the organization of the International Sunday School Association, with its numerous state and county auxiliaries. This was one of the direct antecedents of the International Council of Religious Education.

In the last quarter of the nineteenth century the Sunday school had become so important in the work of the churches that a new style of church architecture was invented and promoted to make adequate provision for its activities. The so-called "Akron plan" may still be seen in many church buildings of today. While the style of architecture suitable for Christian education has radically changed since that time, no church today would think of erecting an edifice without giving some thought to the needs of Christian education. During the same period interdenominational cooperation was achieved in the development of the International Uniform Lessons, providing for the study of the same passage of Scripture in all departments of all Sunday schools on any given Sunday. Today there are several forms of International Lessons, including uniform, cycle graded, and closely graded; and the uniform lesson itself has been transformed to provide for a measure of graded application to the several departments of the Sunday school. The desirability of providing published materials for the Sunday school and of maintaining a measure of cooperation among the denominations in the making of lessons has continued to commend itself to Christian people. It is carried on today through the cooperative lesson-making enterprises under the International Council of Religious Education.

By the beginning of the twentieth century the principle that the needs of the pupils should influence the program of the school had impressed itself upon the Sunday school. It became possible to produce and promote systems of graded lessons and to make provision for gradation of pupils in the Sunday school, with special provision for graded worship and instruction. This interest in the graded church school was crystallized in 1914 by the publication of Walter S. Athearn's significant book, *The Church School.* The tendency today to use the term *"church* school" rather than *"Sunday* school" has significance beyond the mere change of name. It symbolizes the prevailing pattern for this agency, which exists in ideal if not always in fact, that on Sunday morning the church should make provision for a well-organized program of graded worship and instruction, with building and equipment suited to this purpose, with teachers trained for their specific duties, and with lesson materials which are properly adapted for development of Christian living in the light of the maturity of the pupils to be taught.

In summary let us note certain characteristics of early Sunday schools and their relation to the present-day program of Christian education.

1. The Sunday school began as a lay enterprise—founded by a layman, taught by lay people, and held in a dwelling rather than in a church. While some church leaders, notably John Wesley, were quick to see the value of the Sunday school, it is not surprising that under these conditions it made its way but slowly into the life and work of the church. Throughout its development the Sunday school has offered a wide avenue of service to the church's lay people. It has capitalized on the values inherent in having the people of the church be the interpreters of its faith and work. It has, however, failed to take account of the growing need for professional guidance as it has developed in the direction of a more comprehensive educational institution. One of the acute problems of our day is how to preserve the values inherent in lay participation in Christian education and at the same time benefit by the direction and supervision

of those who have made the study of religion and religious education their lifework.

2. In the beginning, the Sunday school was a school for children. The age range was generally from six to fourteen, at the conclusion of which span the pupils were customarily dismissed with the gift of a Bible. However, as early as 1798 a beginning was made toward the extension of the Sunday school to young people and adults, when working women were assembled for instruction on Sunday morning in Nottingham, England. This idea was taken up in Philadelphia, and eventuated in the founding in 1817 of the Philadelphia Sunday and Adult School Union. In due time, an adult Bible class movement was developed, which was both vigorous and widespread. At the height of the Uniform Lesson movement, many churches had achieved the ideal of the Sunday school's being a place for all members of the family.

However, even today the idea persists that the Sunday school is primarily for children. Many churches are unable to develop a vigorous movement of adult Christian education. Most churches sustain a heavy loss of pupils in the adolescent period. The reason for the Sunday school's inability to capture the interest of young people and adults needs extended investigation, and a remedy needs to be found if this historic agency is to continue to serve the movement of Christian education to the fullest extent.

3. The early Sunday school was strongly evangelistic in character and maintained this emphasis throughout its early history. It was utilized by the early church leaders as an evangelistic tool. Most of its friends were

more concerned with winning its pupils to Christ and the church than with the vigorous application of educational procedures.

In more recent times educational method has been emphasized. There are some who feel that the evangelistic purpose has suffered because of this educational emphasis. If it has, this has happened not by design, but because of a misunderstanding of the true meaning of Christian education. The prevailing present-day opinion is that evangelism and education are inseparably bound together, and that in true Christian education they both exist.

4. Early Sunday schools taught much besides the Bible because they were established to provide a general education. This was the only education which their pupils were receiving. With the development of public education, the Sunday schools became more specialized, with a strong trend in the direction of Bible teaching. The curriculum consisted almost exclusively in Bible study, much of it memorization of Bible verses. This emphasis was continued in the International Uniform Lessons, which in the beginning and throughout most of their history were exclusively Bible-centered.

The tradition that the Sunday school must be a Bible school is still currently with us. Modern Christian education has tried to see the needs of the pupil as over against the teaching of subject matter and has found that while Christian nurture will always depend heavily upon Bible material, there are many other types of materials which need to be used. The proper relation between the Bible and other materials is still a problem of current discussion.

5. Robert Raikes and others concerned with the early Sunday schools were primarily interested in persons. It was not their purpose to promote any particular institution. It was the needs of the children of Gloucester which impressed themselves upon Raikes, and his school embodied his best effort to meet those needs.

This interest in people has continued to dominate the Sunday school. Where there has been too great an emphasis on subject matter, this has happened not because of a lack of appreciation for the needs of the pupil, but because of a mistaken notion that those needs could best be met by the teaching of content. A firm pursuit of the principle that the interests and needs of the people to be taught must receive first consideration in planning a curriculum will go far toward solving many of the problems which now beset Christian education.

6. The early Sunday schools were not held in churches. They were not a part of the church's program. It was with some difficulty that many a church was brought to adopt the Sunday school as its own.

This independence of the Sunday school from the church has tended to persist. It has stood in the way of the Sunday school's own highest achievement. Many Sunday schools are held in the church, but have otherwise a very tenuous relation to the church. Many a minister is breaking his heart over the fact that he is finding it so difficult to bring the members of the Sunday school into the church. If Christian education is to achieve its highest purposes, it must be an expression of the entire life and work of the church and must eventuate in leading its pupils into the membership and work of the church. The effort to do this will explain many of the present-day emphases in Christian education.

7. Early Sunday schools made a generous provision of time. As we have seen, Robert Raikes held his first school for five hours on Sunday. However, this tendency quickly shifted to the traditional single hour session. When the primary purpose was one of instruction in the Bible, with only a limited passage of the Bible to be taught on a given Sunday, this was a workable pattern. Under present-day educational theory, however, it is impossible to do the kind of teaching in a single hour which is demanded by a reasonably adequate program of Christian education. Yet most efforts at extension of time have been vigorously resisted by both parents and their children, as well as by the workers. It is true that there are a few instances of church schools held on extended time, but the more customary effort at getting more time is to push the work of Christian education into the week-day. This limitation of time is one of the greatest weaknesses of the Sunday school.

II. THE YOUTH MOVEMENT

Our inquiry into the development of the program of Christian education turns next to the youth movement. During the same years in which the Sunday school was coming into its own, the youth movement was slowly but surely emerging.

The beginning of young people's work within the program of the church is usually fixed as 1881—one century after the beginning of the Sunday school. On February 2 of that year, in the Williston Congregational Church, at Portland, Maine, its pastor, Dr. Francis E. Clark, organized the first Christian Endeavor Society. This society was followed by a second in Massachusetts in the same year. With incredible rapidity, as though it had been born in the fullness of time, the movement spread to England, Australia, Germany, and throughout our own country. By 1887 there were 7,000 or more societies with almost 500,000 members, and Dr. Clark found himself leaving his pastorate to pilot the new enterprise he had so auspiciously launched.

However, it would seem a mistake to suppose that the society was a new invention of 1881. As in the case of the Sunday school, it had its antecedents in numerous previous endeavors to engage the youth of the church in Christian enterprises.

Singing classes or schools, in which youth figured prominently, developed in America during the eighteenth century. There is a record of one in Boston as early as 1717. The extent of this movement is indicated by the fact that sixty singing books had been issued by 1800.

A little later, temperance societies sprang up to combat the ill effects of strong drink. In 1829 a thousand such organizations were counted in New York State alone, with 100,000 members. It seems that young people, and especially young men, played a prominent part in these societies and through them were given an opportunity to band themselves together in an idealistic effort.

Again, the missionary movement, which gathered momentum about 1800 as it expressed itself in a wave of missionary societies, appealed strongly to young people. Some of the names of these societies bear testimony to their appeal to youth, as for example the Baptist Youth's Missionary Assistant Society of New York City, organized in 1806. It appears, therefore, that the famous "haystack meeting" in 1806 was not an isolated event, but an outstanding item in a series which, taken together, helped to pave the way for a youth movement in Protestantism.

There were also during this period youth societies which were primarily devotional in nature. An old constitution of such a society has been preserved from the year 1741. One of its articles, with the spelling unchanged, reads as follows:

> 1 it shall be our endeaveare to spend the tow ourse frome seven to nine of every lords day evening in prayer to gathare by turnes the one to begine and the outhere to conclud the meting and betwene the tow prayers haveing a sarmon repeated whereto the singing of a psalm shall be annexed and ef aftear the stated exersise of the eveneing are ovear if there be any residue of time we will ask one a nothare questions out of the catecism or some questions in divinyty or have some reliagus conversation as we shall best sarve for the edefication of the sosiety.[1]

But the most direct progenitor of the modern youth society or fellowship was the Young Men's Christian Association. Founded in London in 1844, under the leadership of George Williams, a straight line of descent can be traced from it to the first Christian Endeavor Society. The Y. M. C. A. furnished both the impetus and the pattern for other like organizations. It was domesticated in the church in 1860 by Dr. Theodore Cuyler, pastor of the Lafayette Avenue Presbyterian Church, of Brooklyn, New York, with a Y. M. C. A.-type of youth organization within the local congregation. There is evidence that Dr. Clark's organization of the first Christian Endeavor

---

[1]F. O. Erb. *The Development of the Young People's Movement,* p. 23. University of Chicago Press, 1917. Used by permission.

Society in Portland, Maine, was stimulated by an account written by Dr. Cuyler.

Christian Endeavor, being nondenominational in character, made a bid to become the inclusive organization for youth of all evangelical churches, thus in spirit anticipating the ecumenical movement of today. But this dream was soon frustrated. Due to dissatisfaction with the nondenominational character of Christian Endeavor, or to a desire to hold and guide their own youth, or both, it was not long until many of the denominations set in motion youth movements of their own. In 1889 the Epworth League was formed out of already existing Methodist societies. The Baptist Young People's Union followed in 1891, and the Luther League in 1895. Other denominations have followed suit, while still others used the Christian Endeavor as the program for youth work in their own churches.

We have to move well into the present century to find the youth of many denominations once more drawing together decisively in united efforts. The first meeting of the Christian Youth Council of North America was held in 1930, and four years thereafter its program assumed definite form under the caption, "Christian Youth Building a New World." Today the United Christian Youth Movement is an assured fact, with high promise for the days ahead. It is a cooperative effort of the national denominational and national and state interdenominational youth agencies, including in their constituency approximately ten million young people.

A recent development in the field of youth work is the summer conference and summer camp movement. This is assuming great significance both in numbers reached and in effectiveness of program. It has been estimated that there are now 3,000 church camps and conferences, with an attendance of half a million or more.

Today the church without a young people's organization of some kind is the exception rather than the rule. Though differing widely in purpose, structure, and program, youth organizations in general hold these features in common: they include members of both sexes; they limit their membership to persons in the age group of young people; they engage these young people in active participation in program and work; they have a strong religious emphasis, with an accent on evangelism and service; they foster and maintain a bond of fellowship. Basically they all seek to win young people to Christ, to build them up in Christian living, and to train them for Christian service. It is obvious therefore that the youth movement is clearly within the movement for Christian education, and that relationships must be established between it and the other educational agencies of the church.

This integration of the young people's society with the total program of the church is now in process. Most of the denominations are providing for an all-inclusive youth organization, with the prevailing designation "Youth Fellowship." Many local churches have reorganized their work in the youth field to provide for local church youth fellowships, including in the program all the activities of youth in the church.

The young people's society has made many and significant contributions to the program of Christian education. Many Christians today can trace their interest in the church back to the time when they first became active in the youth movement. The society has emphasized the pupil's own participation in program making and presentation at the very time when his increasing maturity has made him able thus to participate. It has emphasized freedom of activity and variety of program, providing for worship, discussion, fellowship activities, recreation, service activities, and contact with outstanding Christians—all of which are important in Christian education. It has often provided a forum for the discussion of controversial social issues and the application of religion to the problems of our time. If these efforts have sometimes lacked depth, and a necessary thoroughgoing study of the bases of Christian belief and social action, this is not an inherent weakness but is due rather to inadequate leadership.

Perhaps the greatest weakness of the society is its frequent separation from the church. Too often it is another organization in the church, with very little organizational or spiritual connection with the church as a whole. This has deprived the young people of the more mature guidance which should come from the pastor and the lay leaders of the church, has served to discourage young people because of their inability to carry their ideals into action in the church as a whole, and has deprived the church of the fresh viewpoint and vigorous leadership which might be expected to come from participation of youth in its total program. A persistent problem which is faced by every church is that of maintaining a vigorous organization for youth which they consider their very own and at the same time keeping young people related to the church as a whole and participating in its activities to the fullest extent of their growing abilities.

III. The Vacation Church School

Next in the line of development of the church's agencies for Christian education is the vacation church school. It is a product of the twentieth century and in its less than fifty years of history has grown to significant proportions. At the present time there are approximately one-fourth as many vacation church schools as there are Sunday schools, and these vacation church schools enroll one-tenth as many pupils as do the Sunday schools. In comparing enrollment figures, it must be remembered that many Sunday schools enroll people of all ages, while the vacation church school enrollment consists primarily of children.

There is record of a vacation church school which was held in Hopedale, Illinois, in 1894. The wife of the minister of the Methodist church, Mrs. D. G. Miles, came to the conclusion that the church school hour was too short, and the time between sessions too long, to give the children a thorough knowledge of the Bible. She therefore hit upon the idea of utilizing the long summer vacation of the children for additional religious education. The school was organized on an interdenominational basis and was held in the public school building. Use was also made of the adjoining park. Mrs. Miles became the director of the school. A fee of one dollar was charged for each pupil enrolled to cover the cost of supplies. Each child was expected to bring a Bible, and if he did not have his own, a Bible was secured for him from the American Bible Society. The school was organized into four divisions with an assistant for each of the divisions. Some activities were for the whole group and some by divisions. These activities included songs, stories, contests, physical exercises, marches, and pantomime. One of the dramatic activities was held in the city park and depicted the wanderings of the children of Israel in the desert. In this brief description we see that many of the characteristics of the present-day vacation church school were anticipated by Mrs. Miles.

The prevailing type of vacation church school had its origin in New York City, though contributory strands have come from other directions. In 1898 the Epiphany Baptist Church of New York held a vacation church school with an emphasis on Bible memorization and Bible stories. In 1901 the Baptist City Missionary Society in New York undertook the promotion of the vacation church school, or the Daily Vacation Bible School as it was then called, with five schools. In 1907 there were seventeen schools. The name of Dr. Robert G. Boville, executive secretary of this organization, is prominently connected with the early development of the movement.

As indicated by the fact that the movement was promoted by a missionary society, the appeal was largely to a missionary motive. It was to take idle children off the streets in summer, bring them into the churches, which at the same time were also unused, and engage them in interesting and worth-while activities. These activities included a large amount of manual work, but there were also Bible study, Bible memorization, Bible and missionary stories, and worship. Home missionary agencies of other denominations were not slow to see the value in the vacation church school and to include it in their programs. In 1911 the Daily Vacation Bible School Association was organized for nation-wide promotion, and Dr. Boville became its first secretary. In 1917 the International Association of Daily Vacation Bible Schools was organized for the extension of the movement into other countries. That the movement has never lost its missionary character is shown by the fact that during the war years it was extensively used in reaching children in communities in which there was congestion of new population because of defense activities.

Concurrently with the development of the vacation church school movement in New York, Rev. H. R. Vaughn, a Congregational minister, had organized a similar type of religious education enterprise at Elk Mound, Wisconsin, beginning in 1898. He introduced high educational standards, a graded Bible curriculum, and utilized teachers who were trained in public school methods and especially coached for work in the vacation church school. The teachers were paid a moderate salary. The schools were held from two to three weeks. The gradation was the same as in the public school, but if there were not more than ten or twelve pupils in a grade, two grades were combined in a single class. These schools served as a laboratory for the training of teachers when held in conjunction with teacher-training institutes.

In Chester, Pennsylvania, Dr. A. L. Latham was, at about the same time, developing another type of vacation church school, which emphasized the sole use of the Bible in the curriculum.

It was inevitable that the vacation church school should be seen as an opportunity for Christian education for the churches and not simply as a missionary outreach of the church. This led to the appointment of representatives of the church boards of Christian education to the membership of the Daily Vacation Bible School Association, its affiliation with the International Council of Religious Education, and finally its merger with the International Council. At the present time the vacation church school movement has been completely absorbed in the general movement of Christian education, with a department in the International Council of Religious Education, and with appropriate provisions for it in the Christian education boards of the denominations.

It is not hard to find the reason for this growing popularity of the vacation church school. In point of time, it adds considerably to the total time available for Christian education. When held for a term of four or five weeks, it equals the time available to the Sunday school in an entire year. It offers consecutive time, with an extended period each day, five days a week, for a period of weeks. This makes possible certain types of educational activities which are difficult to carry on in the Sunday school. It is a vacation-time activity, laying upon its leaders the responsibility for the development of a program which parents and children will regard as an adequate substitute for other leisure-time activities, and thus requiring the use of educational methods of the highest type. It offers opportunity for experimentation in new methods of Christian education, because practice has not yet been crystallized into traditions, as they have in the Sunday school. It provides an opportunity for the pastor of the church to participate in the program of Christian education, which it is difficult for him to do on Sunday morning. It provides an opportunity for a missionary outreach because very often the children not attending any Sunday school will enroll for the vacation church school and in many cases will continue this interest by becoming affiliated with the Sunday school also. Because of its consecutive time it has been able to enlist in its service people who are specifically trained in public school work and for the teaching of religion and thus has in many cases exceeded in its effectiveness the work done in most Sunday schools.

IV. THE WEEKDAY CHURCH SCHOOL

To teach religion on weekdays is not a new idea. The term "weekday church school" is, however, applied to a particular kind of weekday religious education which is held in close relationship with the public school, either during or immediately after school hours, and involves a measure of cooperation between the churches and the schools.

The major reasons for the rise and development of the weekday church school movement may be summarized as follows:

1. It brings religious education into close relationship with the public school program, thus eliminating some of the unfortunate results of the secularization of the public school curriculum. It is argued that when the public school definitely makes provision for the teaching of religion by sharing some of its time for this purpose, and when such classes are held on a part of the public school day, the pupils cannot help but sense the importance of religion and its relationship to all the other subjects of study.

2. It provides additional time for Christian education. Even though classes are held but once a week, and for but a single class hour, throughout the months that the weekday church school is in session the pupils are given at least as much time as is given to teaching in the Sunday school.

3. It provides for a high type of educational work. Leaders of the weekday church school movement have held to the ideal that teachers in weekday church school classes should be at least as well prepared for their work as public school teachers, and in many cases the standard has been even higher. It has also been held that equipment for such classes can be of a higher type when such classes meet either in the public school room, or in churches when only a comparatively small number of pupils must use the church equipment at any given time. It has also been held that textbooks and study requirements can be correspondingly high.

4. It is a means of reaching many unchurched children. Almost without exception, wherever weekday church school classes are held, there are children enrolled who have no other church connection. On an average 25 per cent of the pupils enrolling in weekday church schools have not been attending a Sunday school. Often those children are won to the church, but even if that does not occur, at least a measure of Christian education becomes available to them through their participation in the weekday church school class.

5. It provides the opportunity and occasion for interdenominational and interfaith cooperation. The establishment of a system of weekday religious education requires cooperation between the several faiths represented in the community as they approach the school board for arrangements to dismiss pupils for religious education. On the part of the Protestant churches it usually requires also that they cooperate in a common program so that classes may be held jointly for all Protestant children. It is maintained also that on the

part of the children a better understanding of and a higher respect for each other's faith may be engendered through the provision for religious education in conjunction with the public school. There are some, however, who hold that just the opposite outcome will result, because they feel that dividing pupils in the public school into sectarian groups is undemocratic.

6. It confronts parents with their responsibility for the Christian education of their children. Dismissal of children to weekday classes is always granted only on the request of parents. In a sense, the weekday church school constitutes an arrangement between the school and the parents, with the churches acting in behalf of the parents in the actual holding of the classes.

The first weekday church school was held in Gary, Indiana, in the year 1914. The immediate setting for this school was a unique school program in Gary which occupied almost all the daylight hours of the children in work, play, and study. Feeling the need for more religious education, the superintendent of schools, Mr. William Wirt, entered into an arrangement with the ministers of Gary to provide for periods of religious education on schooltime, under the leadership of the churches, as a part of the regular school day. This sensing of the kinship between religion and education on the part of the superintendent of schools has been duplicated in many other schoolmen. Their cooperation has usually been genuine and hearty and has been no small factor in the success achieved in many a community.

From this beginning the weekday church school movement spread rapidly through its early years. There were many who felt that at last the solution for the American problem of religious education had been found. During the years of the depression there was some decline in interest, and in a number of communities an inability on the part of the churches to maintain the program. In more recent years, however, there has been a marked upswing in interest and extension of the movement. At the present time it is conservatively estimated that there are two thousand communities in forty-six states and two territories which are maintaining weekday church schools, enrolling almost two million pupils.

In the early days of the movement, much discussion was given to the legality of dismissing pupils for weekday classes in religion. A number of famous court decisions have dealt with this problem. In all cases the decisions have been in favor of the practice, provided certain well-established principles involving the state's relation to sectarian education are safeguarded. It is a fairly safe prediction that there are no legal barriers to holding weekday classes which cannot be surmounted by any community which earnestly desires to have them.

The weekday church school offers the church a new instrument for increasing the time and the effectiveness of the Christian education which it is offering its children. Certain difficult problems of integration of an interdenominational weekday church school program with the local church curriculum are evident, and there are few communities which have dealt with this problem in a basic and comprehensive manner.

There are some who maintain that the weekday church school is not the solution for the problem of introducing religion adequately into American public education.

They maintain that in order to make religion truly a part of education it must permeate the whole school program and result in a religious interpretation of much of the subject matter being taught, rather than standing as a separate subject in the curriculum. This point of view will be more fully developed in Chapter VII.

The rapid development of this movement would seem to indicate that in many communities the people have felt that the weekday church school adds an element of great importance to the program of the churches. There is evidence, however, that in some cases the fact of having pupils enrolled in such classes has seemed more important than the quality of work which is done in those classes. The weekday church school movement cannot ultimately succeed unless the high standards announced for it in its initial stages are maintained.

V. OTHER EDUCATIONAL ACTIVITIES

We have described the rise and development of the several agencies which the churches of America are using in greater or lesser degree in their programs of Christian education. There are other activities, however, definitely educational in nature, which fall outside these agencies.

For children and younger adolescents, many churches maintain through-the-week clubs of various types. In some cases the programs for these clubs are determined by the leader in the light of the needs and facilities of the local situation. In other cases use is made of the program of the several national agencies such as Boy or Girl Scouts, Cubs, etc. There is an increasing tendency for these agencies to make provision for church-centered groups of boys and girls whereby the program of the agency may be integrated with the activities of the church. Missionary organizations for children and young people will also be found, though there is an increasing tendency to consider the study of missions a part of the regular curriculum of the church school. Children's choirs also hold an important place in this list.

For high school boys and girls, and older young people, churches often provide such activities as dramatics, recreation, service activities of various sorts, and choirs.

It is in the field of adult work that educational activities will most often be found which do not fall within the agencies that have been described. The increasing interest in meeting the needs of young adults has led to the development of groups for fellowship, discussion, recreation, and other activities which, because of the convenience of the persons involved, often do not come at the time of Sunday school or one of the other organized agencies. Women's work in the church often includes activities which are educational in nature, and to some extent this is also true of men's clubs. Occasional lectures, classes for parents, discussion groups on social issues, leadership institutes and classes, as well as the educational values of service in the church through choirs, committees, and other leadership activities, add a considerable measure of adult education through activities not usually considered a part of the established program for Christian education.

VI. PROBLEMS FOR FURTHER STUDY

The foregoing review has indicated how the agencies for Christian education in the church have arisen in response to a need and usually quite independent of each other. It is but natural that in such a development there should be considerable overlapping of purpose and program. The same constituency is appealed to in a number of them, and the same workers in the church usually need to carry the responsibility for their maintenance. They have served to extend the influence of the church into areas where the needs and opportunities for Christian education were not being met, but in so doing have often been characterized by an independence from the church which has not been to the best interest either of the church or of the agencies themselves.

The time has come when a re-examination of Christian education in the church is imperative. Such a re-examination should on the one hand consider the needs of our day which Christian education must meet and on the other hand evaluate the program as it is now being practiced. This inquiry has been made by the Committee on the Study of Christian Education, whose findings are reported in the subsequent chapters of this book. The areas of study which have been undertaken, to each of which a subsequent chapter is devoted, may be described as follows:

1. *The foundations of Christian education in theology and educational theory.*—Christian education can find its purpose, content, and method only in the nature of Christianity (theology) and in the nature of the learning process (educational theory). Adequate foundations must be found in the light of answers to such questions as: What is the nature of God? How does he reveal himself to man? What is the nature of Jesus—a great prophet and exemplar of the human spiritual quest, or a

final and complete revelation of God, or an actual source of divine power so that communion with him yields a supernatural energy for living? What is the nature of man? What is sin? How does salvation come? How is religious experience acquired and conveyed? What is the purpose of education—to acquaint persons with the Christian tradition, or to relate them to the Christian fellowship, or to make them critically thoughtful in facing their present situations in the light of the past and with reference to the future so that they can be trusted to find their own way? If all of these, how are they to be integrated in a single purpose? What is the Kingdom of God? What is the character of the church?

It has been said that Christian education has not had adequate foundations in the past. If this be true, the reason is not far to seek. As we have seen, Christian education has developed primarily as a layman's movement, but problems such as those listed in the preceding paragraph require the thoughtful consideration of persons trained in theology and education. If it be answered that Christian education has been no more lacking in its foundation than the work of the church as a whole, that still does not excuse it from finding more adequate foundations for the future. Moreover, these foundations must be reconstructed from time to time to take account of new revelation of truth which may have been received through thoughtful study and experimentation in the fields from which the foundations for Christian education must come.

2. *Christian education in the local church.*—We have described the several agencies for Christian education on which the local church depends in whole or in part. When

used by the local church they are the church in action. It is clear, however, that the primary source for Christian education is not to be found in any one or all of these agencies but in the church itself. Too great attention to the agencies may lead to confusion and much ado about very little, without the primary purposes being achieved.

Those responsible for the development of the program of Christian education in the local church must be prepared to answer such questions as: How may persons be happily related to the church from the time of birth and throughout life so that at each stage of their development they may find a true nurture and expression of the Christian life? How can the life and spirit of the church best be utilized in nurturing the Christian life of each person in the fellowship? How can proper attention be given to the greatest needs of growing persons without violating the essential unity of the church itself? How can the several agencies for Christian education be so integrated that each may make a peculiar contribution without overlapping with the others? How can a total well-rounded program be developed without laying too great a burden on lay leadership and available equipment? How can patterns which have fixed themselves upon the church by tradition, but which are no longer adequate, be changed to meet the needs of the present day?

3. *The curriculum of Christian education.*—Whatever may be its basis in pupil needs and its underlying principles, Christian education comes to fruition in the program which is actually developed on the basis of these needs and principles. Guidance is given the local church

in the development of its curriculum through published lesson materials. An examination of current lesson materials reflects the confusion which exists concerning the purpose of Christian education and the way in which Christian experience may be developed.

Lesson materials are tools, means to an end. A tool must be adapted, not only to the purpose for which it is intended, but also to the ability of him who is to use it. What kind of lesson materials would best serve this purpose in the local church?

As we have seen, the educational program of most churches embodies a number of agencies of Christian education. How may a total curriculum be developed which makes proper provision for what is done by these several agencies and at the same time maintains comprehensiveness in touching the major field of study without undue overlapping? How may proper sequence be secured, moving from those things which are most easily dealt with in childhood to the more difficult questions which should properly occupy the study of young people and adults, without such repetition that at each subsequent stage the pupil will feel that he has already covered the material which is offered? How may a proper balance be provided in giving the right amount of attention to each phase of the curriculum of Christian education in the light of the fact that they are of varying difficulty and importance and the further fact that the maximum time available will probably always be inadequate to cover all phases thoroughly?

4. *The place of the home in Christian education.*— There is an increasing awareness that the Christian home is the most important factor in Christian education. How

may a church program of Christian education adequately take account of this? Shall a definite responsibility be assigned to the home? If so, how may the home be motivated to carry its full responsibility? What shall be done with pupils who come from homes that are either unable or unwilling to carry their part of the load? How may the church increase the number of homes which are able to carry their share in Christian education?

With respect to published curriculum materials, shall provision be made for materials to be used in the home? If so, how shall they be related to that part of the curriculum which is to be carried on in the church? If emphasis is to be made on family unity in Christian education, how is this to be provided for in the program of the church without sacrificing the essential values inherent in the grading of pupils in accordance with their maturity and need?

5. *Leadership for Christian education.*—The development of a church program is dependent upon workers who are competent to make it a reality. In the Protestant church Christian education has been primarily a laymen's movement. Are the values inherent in the utilization of lay workers sufficient to justify the continuance of this practice? Should the answer to this question be in the negative, can the church find and train the professional workers needed to carry on this work and finance the carrying out of such a plan?

Should the answer be that the requirements for leadership can best be met by a proper combination of lay and professional workers, what ideally should be the function of each? What should be the place of the pastor in the development of the church's program of Christian education, and how may pastors be trained and motivated to take their share of the work?

How may the most competent lay people in the church be enlisted in the work of Christian education? How may they be given the necessary training to carry on the comparatively difficult tasks of interpreting the Christian religion and developing effective educational processes?

6. *The community and Christian education.*—It is well recognized that in the community in which persons live are important factors in the development of their attitudes, beliefs, and conduct. Thus Christian education can never be the concern simply of the local church. The local church must establish its relationship with the community in which it lives.

How may a program of Christian education take adequate account of the numerous factors in community life which influence religious development? How may agencies in the community which contribute to the Christian education of its people be utilized by the church in the achievement of the purposes of Christian education? How may the church in its turn influence and develop within the community those aspects of community life which will best minister to the highest development of persons?

In most communities there are several churches of several denominations, as well as churches and synagogues of other faiths. How may these local churches relate themselves to each other in such a way that together they may promote the highest aims of each and collectively influence community life?

7. *Overhead organization of religious education.*—In the course of its modern history, Christian education has developed a movement which makes extended provision for the guidance of the local churches and communities in the development of their programs. First in point of origin were the nondenominational and interdenominational organizations for the promotion and improvement of the Sunday school. These agencies now constitute a vast network including local, state, national, and worldwide units. The establishment of denominational boards for the promotion and improvement of Sunday schools did not lag far behind. These boards also have been developed to constitute a vast network of organizations, with numerous professional workers and a wide variety of services available to any local church which is minded to take advantage of them.

Like the agencies in the local church, these overhead agencies have also developed in response to a need. They, too, should be subject to re-examination in the light of the situation before us and the present need. Such questions as the following need to be considered:

How effectively are these organizations serving the local church? How may denominational and interdenominational agencies best be related to each other so that they may cooperate for the most effective service to the church and the movement for Christian education as a whole? What guidance may be given for the future development of supervisory agencies?

These seven areas constitute the fields of inquiry for the study which is being reviewed in this book. A wide variety of persons have shared in seeking a solution to these problems. Their findings will follow in subsequent chapters. The most cursory examination will make it clear that the study has not yet been completed. There are many points at which adequate answers to problems await the results of further research. These findings are presented with a view to the further development and improvement of Christian education. There is one point on which the committee is unanimously agreed and on which probably most church leaders will also agree; namely, the crucial importance of Christian education, and the necessity for carrying it on as persistently and effectively as possible, in the light of our human insight and ability, with the help of Almighty God.

Chapter II

The Foundations of Christian Education

CHRISTIAN education is the process by which persons are confronted with and controlled by the Christian gospel. It involves the efforts of the Christian community to guide both young and adult persons toward an ever richer possession of the Christian heritage and a fuller participation in the life and work of the Christian fellowship. It is both individual and social in nature. It is individual, because it deals with persons, and each person is unique and different from all other persons. It is social, because it seeks to relate persons to the Christian community and to transform community life toward an ever fuller embodiment of Christian ideals. It is concerned with the past, the present, and the future—with the past because it seeks to introduce persons to their religious heritage, with the present because it aims to make religion a vital force in every response to life, with the future because it cultivates creative experience leading to growth in wisdom and stature and favor with God and man.

The foundations of Christian education are to be found in the nature and condition of man who is to be educated, in the faith which the church professes, and in the principles of education which define how learning takes place. These may be examined separately, but the findings from such study will be intimately interrelated in the resulting Christian education.

I. The Nature of Man

Christian education is concerned with the development of individuals into mature Christian persons. It must inquire, therefore, what the nature of these persons is and how they respond to life in the complex world which is their temporal home.

Biology shows us that they start with certain inherited traits and basic human needs. They differ in capacities and native endowment, but these differences are difficult to measure because persons are subject to varied influences from the environment in which they are placed. Some of these influences are deliberately planned by society so as to attain its ends, while many others are wholly unconscious as the individual adjusts to or reacts against the accepted patterns of life. The primary needs of man have a rather definite physical basis and are present in all individuals. The secondary needs are greatly influenced by education and culture.

An enormous amount of study has been devoted to the understanding of man in the various aspects of his development. Physical, mental, social, and religious aspects of development have all been subject to scrutiny. These studies have usually been conducted without religious assumptions or from a frankly naturalistic point of view. Yet, in so far as they help to understand man and his development, these findings are of inestimable value to Christian education.

On the other hand, Christian education has been largely based on definite affirmations about human nature which were originally expressed in prescientific terminology. This does not necessarily make them outmoded. Wide areas of agreement are found between the secular and the religious student. Both express the potentialities of man; both admit great limitations. Where there appears to be disagreement, the Christian educator is faced with the question of how far traditional assumptions must be modified, and the investigator should consider whether he has left out any relevant evidence.

1. *The dual nature of man.*—Man combines a twofold nature within himself. Tendencies toward good lift him closer to God, while tendencies toward evil drag him down. It is believed by some that man has almost unlimited capacity for and freedom in the selection of the good and the rejection of the evil. They believe that man may repress or redirect his antisocial instincts and foster the social ones. Accordingly he is able to respond with devotion to moral ideals when their desirability is shown. They have confidence in human progress. Their hope in developing desirable human beings is based on human teachableness. This is an optimistic view.

But there are others who see a more tragic picture. They insist that reason determines only a small part of human activity. They point to man's capacity for making his self-interest look like the common good. They point out that his conduct is largely determined by deep-lying passions of which he is not even aware. He has within him a war of conflicting impulses. The history of the race shows man as a creature who has been predatory, deceitful, and cruel. When these deep-seated impulses come into conflict with conscience, dangerous repressions may result. Mental illness is widespread among us, indicating that man's spirit needs to be healed as well as his intelligence informed and his will summoned to moral activity.

Christian faith uses language peculiar to religion in describing this twofold nature in man. On the one hand he is a child of God, made in the divine image. Within the bounds of human limitation, he is capable of thinking God's thoughts after him and of seeking to do God's will. God's law is written in his heart, and he experiences a sense of guilt when he disobeys. Though extremely small in contrast with the vastness of the universe, he is capable of predicting the movements of the stars. He bows in worship before his Maker and finds eternity implanted in his heart. Such divine capacities respond readily to nurture within the divine family.

But on the other hand man is also a "fallen" creature. The divine image has been marred. This is the truth which is affirmed in the first chapters of Genesis. There are tendencies to evil in human nature itself so that when man is left to himself he does not find salvation. He is alienated from God by the sin of rebellion. He denies his true nature by his sensuality and pride. He is prone to worship himself and his achievements. His need for deliverance is more real than his need for instruction. It is not enough to exhort him to marshal his own resources, for he stands in need of salvation which can come only through what God does for him. When he experiences this salvation, he knows that it is not of himself, but joyously receives it as the gracious gift of God.

The modern Christian education movement in its early days in this country had a confident belief in the possibilities of Christian nurture for the realization of Christian personality and the achievement of a more Christian social order. In this confidence it was in line with the beliefs of general education that in and through adequate educational procedures the possibilities of man could be developed. The dominant liberal theology of this period also embodied this optimistic view of man. The theological reaction which has pointed again to the more tragic aspects of the human situation has been a disturbing challenge to the assumptions which underlay programs of Christian nurture. One of the greatest needs of religious educators today is to restore the proper balance between these two truths. We should never give up the conviction that we are dealing with the children of God who are growing up within the body of Christ. Man can be sinful only because he *is* a child of God. On the other hand, the empirical investigations which lay bare man's brutality and pride, his sensuality and neurotic characteristics, lend strong confirmation to what the theologians were trying to express through the doctrine of original sin. A sound program of Christian education must take into consideration this dual nature of man.

2. *The predicament of man.*—In his quest for a rich and abundant life man is frustrated by the conditions which circumscribe his earthly existence. One of these is the brevity of his span of life and the inevitability of his death: Does life on this planet mark the bounds of man's existence, or does his being have ampler dimensions? A second is his dependence on nature: Does it contain powers to be appeased, is it a sphere for his mastery, or is it a ground of existence which is friendly to those who approach it with a humble spirit of understanding? A third is his relation to the culture of which he is a part: Is he merely to seek adjustment to the pattern of human culture, or is there a more ultimate frame-

work of existence? These are problems which have always beset man.

Modern life has produced certain new and difficult strains of its own which have intensified man's awareness of his predicament. We are confronted with such a vast expansion of scientific knowledge and technological invention that it is staggering to the imagination. Barriers of space have been so reduced by rapid communication between all parts of the globe that the whole world might become one community, and yet man's wisdom has been unable to grapple successfully with problems of world organization. Human ingenuity has led to a tremendous multiplication of goods but has not produced a corresponding ability or desire to distribute those goods so as to benefit all mankind. Scientific invention has released man from much backbreaking toil but has often made labor so routine and meaningless as to constitute a threat to a feeling of social usefulness and a sense of vocation. Modern science and the machine age have so changed man's outlook on life as to lead in many cases to a substitution of secularism for the historic religions of mankind and an outlook on life which is the opposite to the traditional emphasis on the virtues of integrity, good will, faithfulness, and service. The contrast between the Kingdom of God and the kingdoms of the world was never more sharply drawn than in our day.

These developments in the world in which man lives have set up tensions and conflicts which tear him asunder and often threaten his sanity. They have led to deep fissures and antitheses between races, classes, religions, political parties, and competing ideologies. They have led to a sense of aloneness in the midst of millions of people. They have increased feelings of anxiety and despair. They have led some to be unduly absorbed with external activities and things, and others to try to run away from the struggle through various forms of escape such as commercialized amusement, chronic illness, and a preoccupation with what is considered to be the golden age of the past.

The tensions arising from this predicament of man are not primarily because of external forces pressing in upon him. They are within his own nature. Good and evil are at war within his soul. There is an inner conflict prior to the particular expression of it arising from the immediate social situation. Civilization may increase the occasions for conflicts but it is not their ultimate cause.

In the face of his predicament man may well cry out, "Who will deliver me from this body of death?" Christian faith holds that the solution to this predicament goes deeper than the integration of individuals and their proper adjustment to human society and the world. God is the ultimate reality in man's environment, and the Kingdom of God is the order to which he must find adjustment. Man is a citizen of two worlds. As part of the world of nature he has a physical body. As a creature who transcends nature, he has a soul destined for eternal life. The inner divisions, of which the secular student is also conscious, root in human sin and the denial of the holy will of God.

Man cannot effect his own deliverance but must depend upon resources beyond himself. This redemption does not in fact eliminate all possibilities of the defeat of man's earthly ambition but it does help him to adjust himself to the tragic aspects of life. There is always hope of forgiveness beyond repentance and of a new beginning beyond judgment. No matter how far man may be from God, God is not far from man. Though victory within the world may be denied, there is the possibility of victory over the world. Christianity has never offered a superficially optimistic view of life, nor has it presented God's will as favoring an escape from life. It has pointed a way of salvation by the grace of God to a humanity known to be in dire need.

3. *The contribution of Christian education.*—This is the human situation in which Christian education has its setting. Its responsibility and opportunity are great. It begins with earliest childhood, before persons become too completely enmeshed in the conflicts and tensions of culture, and continues throughout life. With the help of all that has been learned about the nature of man, it seeks to guide growth into Christian channels. If much of the conflict which has been described here is distant from the experience of Christian youth, the reason is to be found in part in the success with which Christian education in home and church has guided them over the shoals and past the rocks of danger. If its failures have been many, it is partly because of the tremendous difficulty of the task and the inadequacy of those who are engaged on it.

Christian education must seek to help persons face their problems realistically. This is necessary before there can be a solution or a discovery of adequate resources. Christian education must seek to help persons to understand the religious heritage and to apply it wisely in the building of their lives. It must do more than seek a recovery of the past; it must call for constructive change toward a better future. Through an effort to enlist persons in remaking their own experience, as well as in the reconstruction of social relationships, Christian education must seek to win a victory for Christian living.

Christian education involves the induction of growing persons into the life of the Christian community. Sometimes there has been a neglect of this community aspect of Christian education because of an undue emphasis on the freedom of conscience and individual responsibility. This has resulted in an unfortunate neglect of social cohesiveness and historical continuity. Just as effective citizenship requires an authentic guide in the moral judgment of the community, so the Christian finds guidance in the stream of corporate experience which the church seeks to embody. In this fellowship of faith the needs of men may be met as they are helped to find effective relation to society, to the world, and to the God who determines the conditions under which man works out his destiny. Thus persons may be led from plight and predicament toward power and peace.

II. The Faith of the Church

The church is the society within which developing persons should grow up as Christians. It is also the body through which the heritage of the past is transmitted. If we conceive it broadly as the people of God, the Bible was written for the church and by the church. It is here that our faith has been formulated and passed on through a living succession of believing witnesses. The church has been the mother of us all, and there is truth in the historic statement, *"Extra ecclesiam nulla salus."*

The church as a fellowship of believers in Christ has a missionary purpose and effect. It cannot hide its light under a bushel but must proclaim the good news to others. It has been zealous in re-creating its faith in its own children. The study of persons reveals the importance of the influence of a group on its members, particularly those who are immature. The impact which has come from this fellowship of old and young in a common faith and a common work has served to re-create in each generation the most cherished convictions of its fathers. The teaching of the young in the meaning of its faith has also been a characteristic effort of the Christian church.

In contemplating the church today the casual observer will be struck by its fragmentation into numerous divisions. Organizational unity is not now a mark of the Christian church, if it ever was. But the modern ecumenical movements are revealing that there are wide areas of common ground among the churches. When set over against the secular alternatives which are bidding for the loyalty of men, such as materialism, the Christian churches are ranged together as members of the same body, the body of Christ. All believe in the living God, the ground of existence and the hope for meaningful life. All believe in Jesus Christ as the focal point of their historic faith. All agree on the basic elements of Christian conduct: justice, temperance, humility, brotherhood, love, service. All agree that there is a people of God which transcends nations, states, and race—a society to which the Christian owes his ultimate allegiance.

These areas of wide agreement should not blind us to the fact that there are sincere differences about organizational patterns and in the more detailed interpretations of the elements of the Christian faith. Nevertheless, they offer basic grounds for fellowship and cooperative endeavor.

If Christian education is to induct growing persons into the life of this fellowship it must recognize that it it dealing with something more than our human quest for the good life. It is sharing in something that is divinely given. We must now turn to the understanding of these elements in our heritage.

Christian faith affirms that *God has revealed himself within history.* A series of acts has taken place in which the redemptive will of God has been manifest. He has spoken through his prophets; his judgment is written in the course of human history; his Word became incarnate for men; and history finds its consummation in his kingdom. Christian experience arises as men respond to that redeeming revelation with trust and obedience. That includes receptive faith and committal to him, active love in the spirit of him who has loved us, and confident hope in the victory of his righteousness and truth.

1. *General revelation.*—"Revelation" is a word which is often used in a much wider sense than this. It is sometimes applied to the fact that God may be known in a measure through the created world. This is fully recognized in the New Testament. When non-Jews are addressed in the Acts of the Apostles, it is assumed that there is a witness to God in nature (14:17). Paul says that the everlasting power and divinity of God are perceived through the things that are made (Rom. 1:20); therefore, all men are without excuse when they worship the creatures of their own hands. The cosmological argument for the existence of God has been built on the fact that God may be known in part through the world of

nature. On the other hand, it is just as true that the nature of God is not to be discovered from this alone.

Again, the word "revelation" has sometimes been applied to the noble insights which have come to men. There is the inspiration of the poet which can never be explained simply in terms of literary effort. The lines come to him in moments of high exaltation. In many religions there have been found various types of mystical experience. The soul of man within has felt that it has been made one with the Soul of the universe without. Sometimes this has accompanied an elaborate spiritual discipline; sometimes it has come to the quiet spirit who sought only to be still in the Eternal Presence. The genuineness of these experiences can be denied by no one who has been taught from the Fourth Gospel that there is a light which enlightens every man. But private experiences must be subjected to social evaluation. Manifestations of the one God must have an inner consistency if they are to be accepted as true revelations.

It is significant that though the Bible recognizes the reality of these experiences, it does not employ the word "revelation" in connection with them. If we make that extension of vocabulary, it should be recognized that we are redefining our terms. We may, for instance, speak of "general revelation," which includes these concepts, and "special revelation," referring to the acts of redemption to which the Bible points. It would be presumptuous to claim exclusive validity for any one use of terms. But it is necessary to remove ambiguity and misunderstanding. In speaking of the divinely given revelation we are using the term in the biblical sense.

The conviction that there has been a revelation of God in history does not exclude the possibility that there are aspects of the Infinite Mystery which are unknown and possibly unknowable. These present subjects for devout meditation and thoughtful speculation. Philosophical systems arise from this very proper speculative activity. Useful as they are to serve the apologetic needs of an age, they should always be looked upon as tentative and temporary. It is not any one of these human philosophies which is the starting point for faith but the historic events themselves which Christian thought should seek to interpret. Our rational systems will always fail to comprehend completely the faith which arises amid a life that is larger than logic.

2. *Revelation in Hebrew and Jewish history.*—The study of Hebrew and Jewish history may be approached objectively, like any other portion of human history. The evolution of their religious ideas and the events of their political development may be traced as we would follow the course of Babylonian or Egyptian history. Such a study shows the differences of Israel's religious experience from that of other peoples. But the value of that difference cannot be established simply by this kind of analysis. We must come to appreciate what these events meant to the Jews themselves: that their God, Yahweh, whom they had at first conceived in quite primitive fashion, was in fact nothing less than the God of the universe. Here we are faced with the need for more than information which is critically sifted in accordance with historical method. We must make a decision of faith somewhere between the possible poles. At one end, some would dismiss the claim as a preposterous conceit; at the other, men recognize the revelation of the eternal God.

The issue is inescapable because the whole Christian development roots in the Jewish faith recorded in the Old Testament. They found here a God who had come into covenant relation with his people. His judgment and mercy were seen in the events of their history. His character was proclaimed by prophets who did not hesitate to say, "Thus saith the Lord." These pages do not primarily offer a theistic explanation of the universe but present One who acts, who redeems, who brings judgment, and who in the end will send his salvation. The foundations of Christian faith are laid in the belief in one God of righteousnes, the revelation of his will in Scripture, and the messianic faith that his purpose must in the end prevail. Here is no distant Being, whom men must seek and feel after; here is One who has acted on the plane of history.

Some find difficulty in the fact that the study of the Hebrew Scriptures shows evidence of their contact with other cultures and other religions. The archaeological discoveries of the last century have illuminated the Old Testament at many points. They have made it clear that Israel's religion did not develop in "splendid isolation" but in living relationship with many cultures of the ancient world, especially the Canaanite, Babylonian, Egyptian, Persian, and Greek. The exact extent of these influences must be determined by the specialists in this field. Theology can never prejudge such an issue. The genuineness of revelation is neither increased by minimizing these influences, nor is it destroyed by their full recognition. The God of the entire universe is not more truly revealed through the experience of a people if it is thought to be hermetically sealed from all outside spiritual influence. It is in the total result that we must find the revelation rather than in the absence of external human stimuli. But Judaism consciously set her face against outside influences at many stages in her development, because she was aware of the difference of her heritage from the religions that surrounded her. That difference is as clear to the student of ancient religions as the truth of her living contacts with her spiritual environment.

Others find difficulty in the moral and spiritual limitations of some parts of the Old Testament. They forget that divine revelation is always and inevitably humanly received. "In many and various ways God spoke of old to our fathers by the prophets; but in these last days he has spoken to us by a Son" (Heb. 1:1-2). No matter how absolute God may be, our knowledge of him shares in the relativities of human experience. The prophet who received the word was not infallible, and the book that preserved the word could not be inerrant, if for no other reason than that it had to be copied by human hands. But though this treasure was received in earthly vessels, the gold is not turned into baser metal by this fact. Consequently, Christian faith is not troubled when it finds different levels of spiritual experience in the Old Testament and lower ideas of God beside the higher. At best, this shows the need for a focus of revelation and a touchstone by which all may be judged.

3. *Christ and his church.*—The focus of Christian revelation is found in Jesus Christ. He is the embodiment of the gospel, the good news of the saving grace and power of God. In him God was reconciling the world to himself. God commended his love toward us in the death of his Son. Here was more than man's utmost devotion to

the divine will. Here was the redemptive act of God himself through a human life in history.

The gospel was first of all a message which Jesus lived and preached. This was more than the good news of God's forgiveness. His own seeking love for the lost was an incarnation of this eternal aspect of the life of God. Jesus proclaimed nothing less than the coming of the Kingdom of God for those who truly repented. In his own ministry, the powers of that rule were already at work, for he stood in a special relation to that kingdom. As "king of the Jews" he was nailed to a cross after his own people had handed him over to the Roman power.

The gospel was also a message which was preached about him. It began with the good news that God had raised him from the dead. Jesus was not only the Christ, God's Anointed; he was their living Lord. They had many ways of expressing what God had done for them in Christ. Sometimes it was in terms of a defeat of the demonic powers; sometimes it was through the analogy of a sacrifice; sometimes Christ was portrayed as the heavenly messenger who had brought life and light from the world above. Some interpretations of redemption were in terms of the original Jewish milieu. As the Christian community spread into the Hellenistic world, interpretations were more in relation to this background. But uniting them all was the conviction that in Christ, God had done everything necessary for the salvation of men that lay within the sphere of his will and power. Christ was not simply one of many mediators between God and men but his ultimate Word for them.

Furthermore, the Christian faith involved a community which centered in Christ. It began with the group to whom Jesus promised entrance to the Kingdom of God. After his resurrection it was the group who looked to him as Lord, and upon whom he poured out God's Spirit. The holy name of "ecclesia" or "church" was appropriated by them. The people of God were not a particular nation, but those from every "tribe and nation and people and tongue" whose new life was constituted through Christ. Through the salvation which was given, the community was established which could appropriately be called "the body of Christ."

This community felt that it had uniquely received the Spirit of God. Belief in the Holy Spirit means that the God of revelation is a living God. Revelation can never belong exclusively to the past if the people of God have truly received his Spirit. The promise was that he would guide them "into all the truth." This did not mean, however, the coming of a totally new and different revelation, for that would deny that Christ has a central place for faith. It meant rather that men would be guided into a fuller understanding of the significance of God's historic acts for men. This has taken place down the centuries. Though a special significance is attached by all Christians to the interpretations given in the New Testament, the later developments cannot be left out of the continuing revelation of God.

4. *Authority in Christian development.*—Authority is the weight that is given by a free person to previous experience other than his own. Major points of difference are to be found among Christians in the extent of authority to be given to Christian history.

Some would regard the church as nothing less than the continuation of the Incarnation, since its development has taken place under the guidance of the Holy Spirit.

Undoubtedly the attempts to clarify and restate the Christian faith have brought new insights. The God who raised up an Athanasius and an Augustine, a Francis of Assisi and a Bernard of Clairvaux, a Luther and a Loyola, a John Calvin and a John Wesley, was one who continued to speak to the generations of men. But the extent to which this involved new revelation is largely a question of definition. It was not a new God who spoke through church councils and outstanding personalities, but these did introduce new acts of the God and Father of our Lord Jesus Christ.

This development involved the utilization of many new tributaries to the original gospel. The categories of Neoplatonic philosophy, and later of Aristotelian, were employed to express the nature of God which was implied in the Christian faith. Ideas from Stoicism were utilized in the formulation of social ethics. Such procedures were necessary if contact was to be made with the thought world of those times. Some claim that the resulting formulation became an integral part of the revelation and are as authoritative as the Bible itself. Others hold that they are only witnesses to the faith and are no more permanent than the thought world in which they were stated.

Does present-day thought contribute to Christian faith? Some feel that though it was legitimate for earlier generations to absorb tributaries for the interpretation of the gospel, Christian faith must stand in complete opposition to the intellectual world of today. Others, on the contrary, feel that it is as much the duty of the church to state her faith in terms of the issues of today as it was in any preceding century. The only necessity is that we state the *Christian* faith, and not some other view even though it be phrased in biblical terminology. For it is not the Christian faith if we deny that man, though a child of God, is a sinful, needy creature, or if we deny that God in his grace and power has met that need through Christ.

Man's understanding of the implications of Christian faith has at times been corrected by movements arising from without the church. For instance, though we assume that Christianity and democracy are allies, for centuries the church was wedded to paternalistic and feudalistic ideals. That is still the case in some branches of Christendom. Democracy has found congenial points of contact with religious insights which have always been stressed. But these implications were not drawn until modern revolutionary movements stimulated their discovery.

Likewise, the Christian faith has at times been supplemented by various aspects of our intellectual progress. A noteworthy example lies in the growth of scientific control and in our understanding of the dependable processes of the world upon which it rests. The faithfulness of God takes on new meaning as experiment reveals our dependence upon reliable uniformities to which we can only adjust ourselves. "Thy will be done" becomes, not a fatalistic submission to all that is, but a utilization of forces which we do not create, for the attainment of a rational good.

Some would go further than this. While recognizing the centrality of the revelation of God through Christ, they believe that new religious insights have come in later history which may actually enrich the Christian faith. For example, they believe that new understanding has come out of psychology, particularly in what has been called mental hygiene, as to sin and salvation; that the social sciences, including the study of history, have furnished data out of which fresh interpretations of what is involved in Christian community have arisen; and that the physical sciences have furnished more accurate descriptions of the nature of the universe and of the world than were formerly available, thus giving new insights about the nature of God and his relation to his world, with significant implications for prayer and worship. While recognizing continuity in the growth of Christianity, they believe that insights of this kind should be utilized as significant contributions to the development and enrichment of the Christian faith.

The divinely given can never be reduced to an idea or to a group of propositions. Such slogans as "The Fatherhood of God" and "The Brotherhood of Man" at best sum up important implications of the gospel. That gospel does not consist in a series of communicated truths but in the saving activity of God which has centered in Christ. The record of that phase holds a unique place as the word of God, but the record is not itself the Word. And without the illuminating presence of God's Spirit, its pages can never mediate the life of God. In the last analysis, it is that which is divinely given.

5. *The function of creeds.*—The attempts of the church to reduce her faith to systematic statements have resulted in creeds. They are an index of the important elements in Christianity at a given time. Usually they are affirmations on the issues that are in controversy at the time and inevitably leave unmentioned many elements of the Christian faith which would be considered vital by many persons. They are prescriptive, in that they mark off the limits beyond which it is fatal for

faith to venture. They exclude those thought to be in error and deny positions believed contrary to Christian faith. However, they do not state all that is significant even to the Christians of the time of their formulation.

The making of creeds began with the early Christians in their expressions of affirmation of allegiance to Jesus Christ. It has continued throughout Christian history and has resulted in certain historic statements of the Christian faith which have been widely used by the churches. In our day there have been attempts to formulate statements of the Christian faith for the ecumenical church.

There is a wide variation in the place assigned to creeds in different church bodies. For some, a creed is a measuring rod to which all must conform. Others look upon it as a guidepost in the expression of faith in relation to particular issues which the church has been compelled to face through the centuries. Some regard them as of historical and informational value only, because of the emphasis which these people lay upon faith which trusts in the living God to give the needed guidance in facing any new issue.

III. Principles of Educational Procedure

How do people learn? This is a third element in the foundations of Christian education. We must go to the findings of the study of persons for our answer. This does not imply that general education can be bodily transplanted into the church. It only recognizes that it is the same person who is to be educated, whether he sits at a public school desk or in a church school chair. If God created him, the laws of his being by which he learns are God's laws. They will operate in the learning of the

Bible and church history as they do in the learning of general history or other subjects.

It is true, however, that Christian education has a special purpose and content, related to general education, but yet distinct from it. It should be free to develop its own method of procedure, based on its understanding of the educational process. Its purpose to develop Christian experience and guide Christian conduct must ever be the test by which it selects educational method.

1. *Continuous growth.*—Education is g r o w t h—in knowledge, in understanding, in emotional maturity, in spiritual grace. Beginning in earliest childhood, growth must continue throughout life. Formal education may end at age eighteen, or twenty-two, or twenty-five, but learning must go on if life is to be lived abundantly.

In the broadest sense, all life is education. The experiences which change life may come anywhere— on the street or in the home as readily as in the school or church. But in a narrower sense, education consists of those efforts and practices through which it is sought to guide growth toward accepted goals. What John Doe is at any particular time in his life depends on all his experience, it is true, but his teachers will have tried to guide that experience into Christian outcomes whenever possible. This conscious effort to guide growth forms the basis of the curriculum.

There are levels of maturity which determine what kind of experience the person can have and the kind of guidance which can be given him. "When I was a child, I spoke like a child, I thought like a child, I reasoned like a child" contains profound educational truth. It has too often been violated by trying to make children talk and think and reason like adults, or to keep young people and adults in the realm of thought and reasoning which are appropriate to children.

Adult ideas of the limitation of childhood experience may be pushed too far. Even a child may experience critical encounter with God, a realization of tragedy in human existence, the impact of moral imperatives, a sense of guilt, the need for reconciliation, the joy of forgiveness, sacrificial love. It must only be remembered that these experiences are at the child's own level and often cannot be made meaningful to him by adult vocabulary.

However, Christian education has probably suffered more from a tendency to force adult concepts and experiences on children. This is due in part to undue confidence in the educational value of indoctrinating children with the verbal expressions of Christian convictions, in part to the tendency in many churches to regard religious education as for children only. There is Christian teaching and Christian experience which is appropriate for children, but some of the far reaches of knowledge and interpretation require the grasp and understanding of an adult mind. This is true in particular with respect to portions of the Bible. Some of the most fruitful pages of Scripture have rarely been opened by Christian education because churches have wanted a single lesson for all ages, or because their young people and adults have not been willing to undertake serious study.

2. *Experience and education.*—True learning is an inward experience through which the pupil appropriates to his own life and character the new knowledge, insight, attitude, or skill in living which may be mediated to him by the educational process. He is like a tree which puts

forth its leaves, blossoms, and fruit because of the inner life which is flowing through it, and not like a Christmas tree, to which others fix tinsel, shiny balls, and lights which are not really its own and never will be.

This conception of learning lays emphasis on the place of experience in the educational process, for experience comes through the person's reaction to life in all the manifold situations which it presents. While it may utilize the contributions of the past, experience is contemporary, and deals with contemporary life, because that is where the individual is living. If learning is to be effective, the things to be learned must have meaning for the learner and be related to his interests and needs. This is not the same as saying that teaching must always follow the wishes of the pupil, for good teaching will be as much concerned with helping the pupil to uncover his own deepest interests and formulate his most urgent needs as with meeting those already recognized. In other words, teaching must always be selective if it has definite goals in view.

Purposeful activity is an important factor in the healthy growth of persons. These purposes accepted as the pupil's own must find expression in activity if meaningful experience is to result. It means little to have a purpose that is not being made explicit in action. Purposes do not mature in storage. Since Christianity is an ethical religion, Christian action is profoundly social. It is a prime responsibility of the church to create and maintain opportunities for purposeful social action in accordance with the highest dictates of Christian conscience. Here again there is need for the initiation and selection of the kind of purposes which are most appropriate for the aims of Christian education. Since the human organism is the most versatile of creatures, this presents no great difficulty.

3. *Growth through crisis.*—Growth occurs both by imperceptible changes and through "red-letter" experiences. There could be no greater mistake than to suppose that the view of education here presented excludes the type of sudden, critical experiences, from which a new base line must be drawn. Indeed, the most significant learnings are likely to be of this sort. Much is made in current educational theory of the problematic situation, the disturbed equilibrium, which compels a fresh adjustment. This corresponds in some sense to the "predicament" of which theologians speak. Significant decisions are taken in that kind of situation where a momentous choice must be made because a forced option is confronted. This consideration has important bearing on the place of conversion in Christian education.

4. *Education and the social group.*—Much of what is learned comes not so much by the direct intention of someone to teach, as through by-products from the general experience of living. Persons tend to become like the people with whom they associate most intimately. Their thoughts, attitudes, and conduct are determined less by processes of study and reasoning than by social suggestion. This is particularly true when the persons concerned are immature and the people with whom they associate are held in high regard.

This aspect of education does not lie outside the work of teaching, but should be incorporated in any larger view of it. Recognizing the importance of social psychology in learning, the educator will wisely provide for group experience in the process which he seeks to develop and control. He will introduce the pupil into groups in which wholesome and satisfactory experiences may be had. Thus we have the educational use of clubs, societies, and the ongoing life of the school.

In light of the importance of the group in achieving educational ends, Christian education has two important resources which it may utilize. These are the Christian family and the corporate life of the Christian church. What these groups are and do is quite as important as what they try to teach, if not more so. Participation in the fellowship and work of a Christian group, coupled with an interpretation of the faith which motivates its life, is Christian education of the highest type.

5. *Subject matter.*—Educators are agreed that subject matter, constituting a record of past experience, should hold an important place in education. But there is disagreement as to just what this place should be. Some would confine the efforts of education largely to the mastery of the heritage of the race, as expressed in history, literature, the fine arts, and speculative thought. In their judgment, this is the best way to give guidance and perspective for present-day living. Others consider it more fruitful to have the curriculum center in current experience. For them the proper use of subject matter is as guidance to understanding contemporary life and in meeting its problems. Both agree that persons in every generation must ultimately come to their own discoveries and interpretations of values and that the expression of the reality discovered by experience may be in terms of acceptance of the formulations of others or of their own creative conclusions. In theory, the difference between these points of view turns out to be largely one of method.

Practically, the divergence turns out to be wider. The first approach is likely to major on transmission of past experience at the expense of genuine inward changes in the pupil. This may go to the extreme of accepting the ability to repeat the formulations of others as genuine religious experience of the pupil's own. The second is likely to fall into the opposite error. It pays lip service to the importance of subject matter but often finds little use for it in teaching. Pupils taught by this approach may be able to form their conclusions on any and all religious problems, but often these conclusions bear only a slight resemblance to Christian faith because the Christian tradition is unknown to them.

This problem is of particular significance in Christian education. Being a historic religion, based on an extensive literature containing the revelation out of which it came, Christianity provides a body of subject matter with which Christian education must come to terms. The place which should be accorded to the Bible, the creeds, and other elements of the Christian tradition constitutes a problem around which most of the controversies concerning present-day Christian education revolve.

IV. Implications for Educational Practice

These three—the nature of man, the faith of the church, and the principles of educational procedure—are the foundations for Christian education. The practice of Christian education which should follow from them will be the theme of the subsequent chapters. It will serve our purpose here to point out a few of the implications for the teaching of religion which follow from the foregoing considerations.

1. *Authority in education.*—The consideration of the use of subject matter has raised the problem of the place of authority in Christian education. Authority in education is the appeal which experience other than his own makes to a free person. It is distinguished from "authoritarianism," a term applied when someone also determines what a learner shall accept, without free choice on his part. This may be accomplished by prescribing what must be believed or by determining what will be acceptable by psychological conditioning.

The question is not one of how authoritative a person's faith will be for himself. Obviously, if it is *his* faith, it will have authority for him. The question rather concerns the extent to which a person will seek to share with his pupil the faith which compels his own allegiance.

The importance of the pupil's own experience in learning tends to the conclusion that no statement of Christian belief will become genuine faith for him until it is an expression of his own inward conviction, based on his own experience. To impress truth on learners by authority from without does not really make it truth for them and cannot lead to genuine growth on their part.

Moreover, honesty in teaching will reject any method which is merely a manipulation of the pupil's mental and emotional processes in such a way as to cause him to accept uncritically what someone else thinks he should believe. It is but natural that the teacher should want to have his own most cherished convictions reproduced in the convictions of his pupil, but he can take little satisfaction in having those convictions merely an echo of his own, with no real rooting in the life of the pupil who professes them.

But it is a mistake to suppose that a pupil can create the Christian faith out of his own unguided experience. It is a part of the business of teaching to share with the pupil those bodies of truth and facts which are relevant to his purpose, so that they may make their own appeal to the mind of the pupil. The Christian faith is based upon and grows out of certain events which occurred in the first century and the interpretation put on those events by those who first experienced them. Christian education cannot do less than present these facts and convictions with all the weight of authority which has gathered around them because of the long Christian history which has been sustained by them and the millions of those who have lived and died by that faith. Moreover, it cannot help but impart these basic Christian convictions with such authority as grows out of their acceptance by the church of which the pupil is a part. Finally, a Christian teacher would be less than sincere if he did not impart the truths which sustain the Christian faith with the hope and conviction that they will elicit faith on the part of his pupil.

There are those who would approach the problem of authority in Christian education by prescribing what must be accepted and believed by their pupils. This point of view is not congenial to Protestant thinking. When all has been done that can be done to clarify the basis and meaning of the Christian faith, and to witness to his own acceptance of it, the Protestant teacher will trust the free response of the pupil.

2. *The use of the Bible.*—That the Bible is central in Christian education is all but universally affirmed by theory and practice. Its place in the development of the Christian faith and in the ministry of the church is so

important that no other position would be tenable. There is, however, a difference of opinion as to the way in which the Bible should be used. So far as this concerns the authority of the Bible, this has been covered in the discussion in the preceding section. There are, however, other questions with respect to the use of the Bible which need to be considered.

The large extent of the literature of the Bible presents the educator with a problem of selection. Because a story happens to be found in the Bible, it is not necessarily appropriate or effective for Christian education at every age level. Harm can even result from using the more primitive elements before the student is ready for concepts of historical development. There are various levels of value for Christian education.

With respect to the use of the Old Testament in particular the following levels may be recognized. The primary level contains those great experiences and teachings which comprise the heart of the revelation of God: his righteousness and mercy, his judgment and salvation, his exalted majesty, and his nearness to those who are lowly in spirit. This core of Old Testament material provides the real reason for studying Hebrew history and religion.

A second level of material adds the historical setting which will make these events and teachings intelligible and which will help to show their real importance. Taken by itself, there may seem to be little religious value in knowing the sequence of the kings of Israel and Judah. This record acquires its significance in relationship to the religious events which accompanied it.

A third level consists of those things which contribute vividness and interest to what is of central importance.

This type of material will include a study of biblical geography and the manners and customs of Bible times. In themselves, these have no inherent value for Christian education any more than the geography of India or the customs of China. But they acquire importance as they serve to clothe with human interest the essential aspects of the revelation.

With respect to the study of the New Testament, and in particular the study of the person and work of Jesus, no one can say that contemporary Christian education has been negligent. The study of Jesus is introduced in some way at all age levels of the curriculum. He is approached from many points of view. Nevertheless, this study leaves much to be desired. Too large a proportion of the time is devoted to the factors which were described in the two preceding paragraphs as having second or third place and not enough to the primary aspect of revelation. This leads to the following conclusions:

In the first place, the career of Jesus in main outline should be more perfectly understood. This involves a larger problem than the question of how we may use him as the example of conduct or the lessons we may learn from a particular saying of his. What was there about the course of his career which made him the central point in God's revelation to man? Seldom is such a project of study undertaken. There have been many courses of lessons on Jesus, but all too often the student has been left without a clear conception of why this life should be more meaningful than all others.

In the second place, the faith of the church about Jesus has usually been inadequately studied. There is no part of the New Testament which does not present him as an object of faith. The apostolic message was the focus for all that the early Christians had to teach. They were not primarily interested in the biography of Jesus; they wanted to proclaim the risen Lord, who had brought God's salvation near.

Undoubtedly the church needs continued experiment in better ways of using the Bible. From the foregoing discussion it is clear that a more rigidly graded use of the Bible must be devised. There are some things which can be done with children; there are many more which must await the more mature understanding of adolescents and adults. It is not enough for us to say that we should have more Bible study. The problem is how its real values may find their place in the lives of pupils, faced with such a bewildering variety of experience. When we view the lamentable ignorance of the Bible in the churches of today, it is difficult to defend the adequacy of any of the current efforts.

3. *Christian history.*—Present-day Christian education largely disregards the Christian development down the centuries. There is relatively little attention given to Christian history or to the outstanding personalities of the church.

This neglect has tended to leave the pupil without a sense of continuity between the people of God in the Bible and the people of God as represented by the present-day church. The values which should come from the pupil's being a part of a great historical movement have been lost.

Moreover, preoccupation with the teaching of the Bible indicates an inadequate conception of what is involved in Christian education. It offers an unbalanced curriculum. Many historical characters who have lived since Bible times may be just as inspiring for Christian living as some biblical figures. There are events in the history of the church which are more important for a modern Christian than some of the events of Bible history. For example, does not the inspiring story of Adoniram Judson, and others of the great missionary and social leaders, contain more value for Christian education than the account of the campaigns of Joshua? The God of history did not die with the completion of the canon of the Scripture.

4. *The church.*—The church serves as an agent for Christian education, not simply by what it teaches, but by what it is.

There is value for Christian growth in participation in what is known as the "cultus," the practices by which the spiritual life of the church is carried on. Churches differ in their acceptance or rejection of the observance of the sacraments, liturgical usages, the traditional Christian symbols, the observance of the Christian year. The mood of today is in the direction of their wider use. Churches which accept such historic practices claim for them great utility as deepening church consciousness. Christian education itself, in such churches, relies less on merely intellectual disciplines or presentations of Christian truths and more on the subtle influence of participation in cult activities and familiarization with symbols.

There is value for Christian growth, also, in participaton in the activities by which the church maintains itself and does its work in the world. The full force of the doctrine of education by participation bears on this point. Churches have sought to find projects in which to engage their children but have too often overlooked the most significant projects of all in the work which it must do to deserve to be considered a Christian institution. It is the common life of the family with its sharing of work and privilege which makes the home most educative. Christian education might profit greatly if the leaders of the church would do less *for* children and young people and do more *with* them. There are limits to the extent to which the making of decisions by the church group, and the consequent work to be done, can be shared by its younger members, but those limits have rarely been even approached by most churches. This would be "life-situation" education of a high order.

5. *Contemporary experience.*—The need for carrying on Christian education in a framework of present experience in order to make it vital for the learner has already been discussed. For any person, religious experience is always personal and contemporary. He may study the experience of the past and the generalizations in Christian doctrine which have been built upon it. Through such study he may the better understand his own experience and evaluate its significance. But for him Christian education must involve a vital experience of his own as he seeks to come to terms with his own life situations if it is to be more than a mere study about the religion of others.

Our concern here is to recognize the value for the curriculum of contemporary life with which the pupil is surrounded. If we agree that there is a general revelation of God, there is need for asking what God is saying today through the world about us. Once the teaching of the Bible concerning God as the creator is accepted, the world which he has made becomes a fitting object of study for all who would know the Supreme Artist. Those who would limit the curriculum to biblical material need to explain how they square this position with the teaching of the Bible itself.

Again, the conviction that God is to be found in individual inspiration and mystical experience provides a basis for including lessons which center about contemporary experience. It is the essence of Christian education to lead persons into an experience of God and the knowledge of being accepted as his children. This is evangelism. By some it is achieved by a climactic experience of conversion. To others it comes without marked crisis, through nurture in the Christian home and the church. However initiated, the commitment of life to God is not usually limited to one transforming experience but is an ongoing process through life. The highest educational art must be applied to the achievement of this end and to it the whole curriculum must contribute. It is not something which a teacher may do *for* his pupil; the teacher is but a humble instrument in helping to provide the situation through which his pupil may meet God.

Opportunities for this are found in the Christian nurture which seeks to lead the pupil to live his life constantly in the presence of God. They are found, also, in resolving the strain that is built up by deliberate wrongdoing, the prolonged denial of religious promptings, the tragedy of deep involvement in sin. The experience of repentance and return to God is not outside the educational process and certainly need not be limited to the adult level. Opportunity exists also in the interpretation of social issues in the light of religion. God is active in world movements of today as well as in the past. As youth and adults face their life problems and the problems of the world, and think through these issues in the light of the gospel, divine guidance may confidently be expected. The living God continues to manifest himself to his children. His voice may be heard now, in the experience of those who are attuned to it.

Chapter III

The Church's Program of Christian Education

*T*HE communication of the Christian faith is a joint responsibility of the home and the church. The work of the home will be more fully considered later, while this chapter will deal with the program of the church. It will touch the home only where desirable relations between the home and the church should be considered.

It is only as local churches grow in numbers, improve in quality of life, and increase in effectiveness as teachers of the Christian faith that the aims of Christian education will be realized. Vast organizations, such as assemblies, conferences, and councils, with their boards and committees, their millions of adherents, may be more impressive than any local church. These associations will give guidance and strength to the local units. But the real strength of the church is in the quality of the Christian life as it is lived and taught in the local congregations.

The church communicates the Christian faith in two important ways: (1) by its spirit and life, and (2) by its more direct efforts at teaching. Its entire life, as it seeks to come to the full realization of the fellowship of those who love the Lord Jesus Christ and by its work to do his will, is a transforming influence in its adherents. To this is added the effort by which it seeks to make explicit and interpret the Christian faith through more direct teaching. This involves the holding of classes, a time and place for teaching, teachers, curriculum materials, and such activities as are appropriate to teaching and learning. These two are inseparably related. The first without the second places too much dependence on immature persons for assimilating and understanding its richness of meaning; the second without the first is impractical and to a large extent futile.

I. CHRISTIAN EDUCATION THROUGH CHRISTIAN FELLOWSHIP

The church is such a body that from its spirit, life, and work there is an influence which flows into its members. In common with other social groups, it exists in time and space. All such groups tend to exert an influence on their members which causes them to share the group's ideals and loyalties. But the church is distinguished from other groups in its conviction of divine origin, its existence in both time and eternity, and its sense of unity with all other church groups through a common loyalty to Jesus Christ, *the* Church, the body of Christ in a temporal world.

In New Testament times, the condition for entrance into the fellowship was a personal faith in Jesus Christ as Savior and personal loyalty in discipleship to him as living Lord. This meant a new life in the Christian group, in which each person felt himself to hold a trust for all his fellow members. It was a bond stronger than the natural ties of family, culture, race, tribe, or nation. So today, membership in the fellowship should involve commitment to a faith and a way of life which is characteristic of the fellowship. It should mean discipleship to a living Lord, with an earnest effort to learn from him as well as from others.

The church unites its adherents in such characteristic activities as worship, fellowship, study, and service. But the church is more than these activities through which it seeks to express its life. The church is its people, their lives in homes, in their social contacts, in their work, and in their play. Wherever the life of the fellowship impinges upon and transforms the life of every day, there is the church. It is the quality of its life in all these phases that most powerfully teaches children, young people, and adults, both within and without the fellowship.

In this fact lies the significance of the Christian home. In the daily intimate contacts of the home, the Christian fellowship has its greatest opportunities and responsibilities. Every member of the family, young and old, shares the responsibility for making this fellowship a genuine church of Christ and through it receives the spirit of Christ flowing into its members by the grace of God.

Entrance into and life within the Christian fellowship are basic in Christian education. The sense of belonging and the sharing of responsibility provide favorable conditions for growth. From his earliest contacts with the church, and as fully as he is able, the child should have a sense of his own belonging to the fellowship. To him, his membership in the children's groups is, in a very real sense, membership in the church. And so it should be, for every group maintained by the church, for worship, study, or fellowship, is a manifestation of the life of that church. From such beginnings growth toward full fellowship may progress in an orderly way.

Through its worship and work, the Christian community opens its life to its more immature members and shares with them the ideals, beliefs, and activities which dominate the fellowship. This is the church's most effective way of teaching. It requires forethought, so that results may be not simply accidental, but designed. It requires a plan whereby the less mature may be enabled to grow into more and more mature participation.

1. *Growth in consciousness of membership.*—From the simple contacts in childhood to the fullest sharing in the fellowship in maturity, the path should be clearly marked. The journey along this path should be definitely planned. There is a place in the church for the child—the largest place which he in his immaturity can occupy. But as he grows older he must progressively put away childish things. He should have a clearly defined status at each stage of his growth. He is not only *in* the church but also *of* the church—not yet a full member, but nevertheless with a definite place in the body of Christ. About the time of adolescence, he is prepared to take the vows of loyalty on his own responsibility. But even this is not the end of the process. Continual growth should mark more and more mature participation in the fellowship. The church on her part should celebrate each successive stage of growth as it is reached by fitting ceremony, by the assigning of greater responsibility, and by providing continuing study so that advancement in participation may be accompanied by corresponding growth in understanding.

This process of growing up in the fellowship will be accompanied by instruction in the meaning, message, and mission of the church. Such instruction may be intensified in a special period of preparation known as the pastor's class or the church membership class. But instruction in membership must be a continuing process, beginning long before the membership class, and continuing throughout life. In a sense, the whole curriculum is a curriculum of church membership.

2. *Worship.*—This principle of learning through sharing is most clearly seen in participation in worship. The most characteristic act of the church is the worship of God. God himself has created in man the capacity to answer the impact of his Holy Spirit on man with an attitude of humility, gratitude, reverence—in short, worship. There is no activity of the church which can so readily include the participation of all ages as public worship, nor any which will give the entire church family so much a sense of oneness. Moreover, in the hymns, the prayers, the responses, the Scriptures, and the discourse, all performed in an atmosphere of reverence, there is a revelation of the character of God as well as the means of communion with him.

It must be recognized that it is not possible to arrange a general service of worship which equally well meets the needs of all ages. To attempt this leads inevitably to grading it above the abilities of younger children. To do otherwise would be to lose some of the more mature expressions of religion which are needed by the adult members of the congregation. But even these elements may provide an experience which familiarizes the children with words and practices which are learned through the very act of participation. Thus worship, engaged in because it is the highest realization by the Christian community of its spirit and object, is at the same time its most powerful influence in the establishment of the religious attitude. But, to achieve these values, ministers need to plan the general service of worship with the presence of younger members definitely in mind.

There is need also for graded, departmental worship. These departmental services will give children and young people of approximately the same age the opportunity to express their religious feelings in the forms of their own experience and in fellowship with each other. They offer a fruitful opportunity for younger persons to learn the meaning of worship.

Worship is a natural impulse, but its forms and expressions are learned. The teaching program must assume as a major responsibility the teaching of young and old in the meaning and forms of worship. Here again we see that Christian education involves practice in the act and instruction in the meaning of that act as inextricably interwoven.

3. *Work.*—Learning through participation may come also by sharing in the work of the church. This is performed through officers, committees, service groups, and individual acts of members. Such service in the work of the church is an important avenue to understanding the meaning and purpose of the church as it seeks to communicate and express its Christian faith. Training for such specific acts of service is an important and effective phase of Christian education. In the performance of these acts, officers and committee members are helping others more fully to understand the meaning of Christian life and work.

Educational strategy has still to devise effective means of introducing the younger members of the church family into its purpose and program. Present practice concentrates on doing things *for* children and young people, rather than allowing them to do things *with* the entire church group. This presents a difficult problem. Some light in its solution may be gained from good family practice. Christian families desiring to practice democracy in family group life have succeeded in a measure in allowing even the children to have a share in planning and work. While the younger persons in any society are usually in the position of receiving more than they contribute, there is a "growing up" value in sharing as fully as possible in the significant activities of the group.

II. Christian Education through Teaching

Thus far, consideration has been given to the values for Christian education in participation in the Christian fellowship. We have seen how guidance and interpretation are needed at every point to make the activities of the church most meaningful in the growth of the participants. We turn next to these more specific efforts at Christian teaching. These two things are not parallel in the sense that either the one or the other might be utilized. They are inseparably united in Christian education at its best.

A comparison may be drawn with community life. The life of any community, in its homes and stores, on its streets, and on its playgrounds, gives education to every child. The community, however, maintains a school because there are many things to be learned which general community life does not teach. They include the common tools of communication, such as reading and writing, guidance in the practical and moral problems involved in human relationships, exploration and interpretation of the life in the community, extension of experience beyond the community into world-wide relations. Just as the community needs the school for these purposes, so the church needs to accompany the experience which comes through opening and sharing its life with its more immature members by a program of instruction, interpretation, and guidance.

The teaching program of the church requires that some of the more mature members share their fuller understanding of and commitment to the Christian faith with those who are less mature. It calls for classes, discussion groups, opportunities to practice Christian living. It utilizes books, lesson materials, pictures, maps, and equipment of all sorts. It employs classrooms, time schedules, and organizational arrangements. All these teaching activities taken together constitute the church school. It may include any or all of the agencies which have been developed for this purpose, as described in Chapter I, and other activities which do not fit into any of these agencies. These teaching-learning activities are for young and old, for all must undergo the discipline which alone will yield growth in knowledge, understanding, attitudes, and skill in living the Christian life.

The point of view which has thus far been developed is that the church itself is the only adequate agency of Christian education. It may express itself through and utilize the several agencies, such as the Sunday school, the young people's society, the vacation church school and others; but it is only as these agencies are integrated into the total pattern which is the church that Christian education can become truly effective.

While traditionally the educational work of the church has expressed itself through certain agencies and patterns, the important thing is not the maintenance of any given agencies, but the meeting of the educational needs of the congregation. This will often require new and better patterns of work. Whatever plan of organization may be worked out for any particular local church, it is important to maintain the point of view that it is the church in action and that it does not have any place or status apart from this.

III. ORGANIZATION FOR CHRISTIAN EDUCATION

The development of a program of Christian education such as has here been described will require drastic rethinking of organization. New patterns need to be developed through which the program can function. Organization will always be secondary to program, for it is but the structure which makes the program possible. But it is just as true that a faulty structure may lead to ineffectiveness of program.

Due to many factors, which vary in different churches, there will probably be a wide variety in forms of organizations which will be found satisfactory in different churches. It is desirable, therefore, that we begin with certain principles which must be embodied in any effective organization.

1. *Characteristics of good organization.*—The pattern of organization which will best serve a church in developing its program of Christian education will include the following characteristics:

a) Comprehensiveness. It must be able to take advantage of all the activities of the church through which Christian growth may be achieved. It must be able to include every member of the church's constituency in its program. It should enable the leaders to plan a balanced program for each member in the constituency, utilizing any and all the existing agencies and activities and devising new ways of achieving desired results when old patterns do not serve.

By way of example, let us take a fourteen-year-old boy in a given church. What provision should be made for his Christian education? At some point in the program-making process, it should be possible to consider his needs and plan accordingly. This will require the utilization of whatever can be contributed by the Sunday school, the youth group, the weekday school, the vacation church school, the church membership class, the church service, and his home. Each of these must be guided in doing for him what it can best do. No one agency can adequately plan for him. What is required is a perspective which comes from a group which can see the program in its entirety and guide each individual factor. They must all be seen as the total church program in action with and for this one person, in the light of his present and future needs.

b) Unity. It is not enough that the various programs in which our boy participates should each make a vital contribution to his education. These several contributions must be worked into a single pattern which has unity. To accomplish this requires an organization through which the leaders of the church can develop the total purpose of the church as it touches its constituency and plan a program accordingly. This is not contrary to variety in program. A body has many members, but they do not vie with each other for importance. Rather each in its own way serves the needs of the whole body. Any person may engage in a variety of activities, but somewhere in the overhead planning there is unity and purpose in it all.

c) Grading. One of the things which the church and the family have in common is their inclusion of people of all ages. This involves the obligation of serving each in accordance with his needs. Education has firmly established the principle that to be effective, teaching must be within the comprehension and interest of the pupil. It remains for the church to work out this principle in the light of its maintenance of the inclusive Christian fellowship.

There are some activities in which togetherness is desirable. We have already seen how this is true of public worship. Increasing numbers of churches are trying to work out a pattern of public worship which makes possible maximum participation of old and young. In some cases this takes the form of a general service which has a wide range of appeal and in which all share. In other churches the plan is for periodic "family" services, which are especially arranged by content and length to include satisfactorily all members of the family except perhaps the youngest. Still others have worked out a unified type of program for the entire Sunday morning, which is "a church and only a church," including worship, instruction, and sermon. In this there will be some period during which all are together in the church sanctuary and some provision for graded activities. Young people and adults usually participate in a full length "church service," followed by division into graded classes, while younger people go to their graded groups at an earlier point in the service, preceding the sermon.

Some attempt has also been made to join young and old more completely in the work of the church. In some cases this takes the form of a constitutional requirement that younger people must be on all important boards and committees except those required by law to have members of legal voting age only. In others there has been joint discussion of important issues of church program. Still another way is to bring to groups of younger people for discussion such important matters as budget, building problems, and missionary activity. Many service projects in which the church is engaged may be shared by persons of all ages. Church-night programs for fellowship, study, and worship also provide an opportunity for joint participation of young and old. Father-son and mother-daughter dinners are a step in the direction of bridging the gap between the ages. Play activities, such as picnics for the whole church, might well be more widely used. Many families have found that there are some recreational activities in which the whole family can share. Can we not make similar discoveries for the church family?

Manifestly there are limitations in the application of this principle, but good church organization for Christian education will provide for applying it as far as possible.

There are other activities which can best be carried out in graded groups. This includes instruction, graded worship, certain types of service, and most of the recreational activities. In small churches the grading cannot be as close as might be desirable, and no amount of "practical" wisdom can overcome the fact that such grading is necessary. It is a penalty which must be paid for Protestantism's division into many denominations. It cannot be denied that the small church has certain advantages in the matter of fellowship and individual attention from the minister, but effective age-grouping is not one of them.

d) Authority. The board or committee charged with planning and carrying out the program of Christian education should have authority to function in all areas where it must do its work. This does not mean arbitrary or dictatorial power. It does mean, however, that authority to do a job of work is delegated, with the necessary power to carry it on. This authority is given by the church itself, and the need for it makes it clear that no self-constituted or self-perpetuating group can serve in this capacity. Moreover, this planning board or committee cannot be set up by one of the agencies, such as the Sunday school. It must be representative of the whole church, with power to supervise the several agencies which constitute the church's program.

This authority for the central body which plans and supervises the program of Christian education is not so difficult to acquire as it may at first seem. Undoubtedly there will be on it some of the leaders of the different auxiliaries of the church. When these auxiliaries see that this plan of organization is not a hindrance, but a help in achieving their aims, there will be no sense of competition for authority. Each may well see the opportunity for cooperation in the achievement of the highest purposes of the church. If there are auxiliaries who regard their own prerogatives as more important than the welfare of the church, it is clear that the time for reorganization has come.

e) Distribution of leadership. When Christian education is properly organized, it distributes widely the responsibility for the communication of the Christian faith within the fellowship. This will make available for the service of Christian education the various talents and interests of different members of the constituency. It will avoid the overworking of a few faithful persons. Thus it will provide many persons with the discipline which comes from service to the church. There is perhaps no more important way for vitalizing the Christian faith in persons than the responsibility for communicating that faith to others.

f) Adequate budget. When Christian education is regarded as not merely an adjunct, but a part of the main business of the church, it follows that it must share adequately in the financial resources available for the work of the church. The kind of program here considered cannot be carried out with the offerings of the pupils in the program. Nor is this desirable. The offerings of pupils in the church school should be contributed to the causes represented in the total church budget, so as to constitute training in Christian giving. Better still, there should be a single budget and a single offering from each person, if the principle of unity is to be maintained. Since we are prepared to regard all the activities as the church in action, each person may present his offering for a given week at any one of the services in which he participates. The church's budget should in turn provide for adequate financing of the church's whole program, including the various educational activities. Such a plan for Christian giving will provide a good basis for education in Christian stewardship in the giving of money, and such education will on its part help in maintaining an adequate budget.

2. *Organizational structure.*—What type of church organization for Christian education will best embody these characteristics? Two major types of organization have been proposed. The first has been practiced ex-

tensively, the second is not so common. The effectiveness of each will depend not so much on its perfection on paper as on the spirit in which it is practiced. There are forms of each which closely approximate the other.

a) One of these is the board or committee of Christian education plan. This provides that the church erect a board which shall be given responsibility for all Christian education activities in the church. It will study the needs of the church and the community and the resources with which to meet those needs. In the light of this study it will project a program which will touch not only the children and young people of the church but the church's entire constituency. It will utilize the existing organizations of the Sunday school, youth fellowship, vacation church school, and others, but it will seek other ways in which parts of the constituency not adequately reached by those institutions can be touched with effective Christian education. It will integrate these several strands into one comprehensive church program.

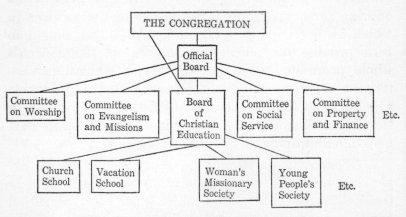

Nevin C. Harner, *The Educational Work of the Church*, p. 65. Used by permission.

The strength of this plan is that it sets aside a responsible body for the development of the whole program of Christian education in the church. Its weakness lies in the fact that a board or committee of Christian education must be paralleled by other boards carrying other interests, such as missions, social service, worship, stewardship, and therefore is put in a position of competing with other interests in the church. It is obvious, for example, that missions should not be made a parallel interest with Christian education, for Christian education without missions is not complete Christian education; and missionary activity without education in missions is likely to be limited to a few who have become missionary-minded in some other way, or else become merely a matter of promoting missions.

b) The second plan calls for a general planning board for the entire church. It assumes that Christian education must be included within the total interests and activities of a church. It provides therefore for a board of strategy which has in charge the planning of the entire church program, including Christian education. In this planning body the various interests will be represented, such as missions, stewardship, social action, and Christian education. There may be special committees on each of these interests, but they do not approach the constituency directly, seeing rather that their interest is adequately represented in the total plan and program through the general planning board. This plan has the advantage of putting Christian education in proper perspective, without setting it apart as a separate function. It has the disadvantage that a general planning board may submerge education because of the many and varied interests with which it must deal.

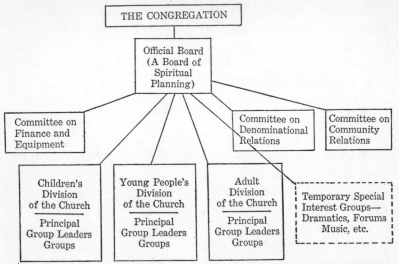

Nevin C. Harner, *The Educational Work of the Church*, p. 70. Used by permission.

Under such a general planning board, by whatever name it may be called, it is possible to charge a subcommittee with all the church activities for children, another with all the activities for youth, another with all the activities for adults, and still another with the development of a program for church help to the home. Thus may the Christian education activity of a church become an integral part of its total purpose and program, the needs of each person in the constituency be adequately considered, and agencies and auxiliaries utilized for what contribution they may best make.

It is not our purpose to recommend one or another type of organization. Much will depend on what is possible and desirable in a given church. There are no doubt many ways in which local or denominational plans can be worked out to satisfy the requirements of the ideals here set forth. We do, however, go on record as unqualifiedly opposed to the separation of the church's program into such separate and independent parts as the church service, the Sunday school, the young people's fellowship, each with its own constituencies and loyalties, without adequate integration into a total program.

For convenience we shall hereafter refer to this central planning group, whatever its type, as the board of Christian education.

3. *Leadership.*—The operation of a well-organized program requires effective leadership. This is especially true when the work is to be distributed among many people. There needs to be a guiding head for the whole organization, with clearly defined relationships with those in authority over departments. This person must see the whole purpose and program of the church and the educational program in all its phases.

The minister is the one person who can and must assume this position of leadership. Historically the Christian education movement, as represented in the Sunday school, was a lay movement. Inestimable harm has been done to the movement by the inability or unwillingness of ministers to take leadership in it, or the unwillingness of laymen to allow them to do so. The time has come for the minister to assume his educational function. He has, or should have, adequate training for this purpose. No one else is in such a strategic position to give leadership to the whole church program as the minister.

Most churches are unable to provide for professional leadership of any of their activities apart from the minister. There are some, however, who are able to employ an associate, man or woman, whose specific responsibility is for Christian education. This associate will be specifically trained in Christian education and will assume the more technical aspects of the job, devoting his time primarily to the teaching program of the church. This does not mean, however, that the minister is then relieved of all responsibility for Christian education. He must still be the head of the staff, the one who sees the whole program in all its aspects, including Christian education.

There is here no intention to minimize the place of laymen and laywomen in Christian education. They have always had, and probably always will have, a large place in it. In this, as in all phases of its work, the church will make the widest possible use of lay leadership. Usually there will be a lay superintendent, who will have immediate responsibility for the Sunday school, in close association with the minister and under the supervision of the appropriate board. In most cases this lay superintendent will not have the time or ability to give executive direction to the whole program. Hence there will need to be corresponding and coordinate leaders for the vacation church school, youth work, and other activities. In churches where a divisional plan of organization has been worked out, there will be laymen and laywomen at the head of each of the divisions, again in close association with the minister and under the supervision of the board of Christian education. In positions of lesser scope, but not lesser importance, there will be numerous men and women and young people of the church.

It is the tradition in Protestant churches that these lay workers will serve on a voluntary basis. However, the practice is increasing of paying persons in key positions a stipend for their services, when this is necessary to help them make the proper preparation, give adequate time, and be relieved of other necessary duties. There should be no more objection to this than to paying a church organist, janitor, and others who are expected to give an amount of time beyond their ability to contribute on a voluntary basis.

The problem of leadership for the work in Christian education will be fully discussed in Chapter VI. It should be pointed out here, however, that all these workers are representatives of the entire church. Their appointment should be made by the proper church board, and their service recognized by the church through appropriate services of consecration and recognition.

4. *The age groups.*—The plan of organization thus far developed will present the following picture, so far as the several age groups in the church are concerned:

For the *children* there will be a single division of the church, with unified program and leadership. There will be no special organizations for children to further specific interests. All the interests of children will come to expression through a unified program. The needs of the child take precedence over organization. The child is in the church—sometimes in the Sunday school, sometimes in the church worship service—but never in an independent children's group unrelated to the church and its program for childhood. The child needs worship experience and training in worship, instruction in the Bible and the Christian faith and tradition, guidance in Christian living, an understanding of the church and a growing experience in its life and work, service opportunities, and social experiences. There is no reason why these needs should be met by half a dozen independent organizations; a single, well-rounded program under the direction of the church will do it better. For these are children of the church.

The *youth* of the church will also have a single, comprehensive program. All too often the church has permitted a twofold or even a threefold appeal, urging them to "join the young people's society" and to "come to Sunday school" and to "join the church." Often the programs themselves have overlapped. Organization has been given precedence over persons. Instead, there needs to be planning for all the needs of all the youth of the church. It is inevitable that some young people will exercise the elective privilege and select from the activities offered those which appeal to them most, either inherently or because of the time at which they are held. But adults work on this principle also. This fact is no argument against comprehensive planning and unified administration.

Increasingly, churches are organizing their young people as a "youth fellowship," including all in the constituency who are of appropriate age. This is a wholesome tendency, provided only that it is developed in the light of the principle of desirable relationships with the entire church, which has been emphasized earlier in this chapter.

The organization of *adults* presents a more complex problem. In large measure the adults *are* the church, as represented by its boards, officers, and committees. They also have the largest representation in the general worship services of the church. We have recognized that these aspects of the church's program have educational significance. Thus, if we did not go beyond this point, we should have Christian education for adults.

But this is not sufficient. Adults also need classes, discussion groups, work projects, and other activities which are specifically designed for Christian education. Of the several agencies for Christian education, the Sunday school is the only one which has traditionally included adults. But in large numbers of churches there are no adult classes. This is not as it should be. For many, Sunday morning offers the best opportunity for attendance at classes for study and instruction. Moreover, a strong adult constituency will give strength and morale to the Sunday school.

There are other opportunities for adult Christian education. There is a growing tendency for young adults to organize themselves around their own interests, and often they meet at other times than the Sunday school hour. Women's groups and men's groups should include educational elements in their programs. The use of religious periodicals and books for private reading is a wide open field.

These considerations make it clear that in the case of adults it is also important that there be a comprehensive approach to program planning. When and where these educational activities are held is not important. What is important is that the adults of the church continue under its program of Christian teaching. A central planning group will utilize existing agencies as fully as possible and will devise new activities when necessary.

IV. What Becomes of the Sunday School and Other Agencies?

This chapter on the organization and program of the local church for Christian education might end at this point. It is desirable, however, that something be added about the use of the agencies of Christian education whose development was traced in Chapter I. We have presented a new approach. We have assumed throughout, however, that the contributions of these several agencies will be integrated into the new plan. How this may best be done depends on the lasting values which each has to offer. No attempt will be made to offer detailed suggestions for the operation of these several agencies. For such help the reader is referred to the voluminous literature which is already available on how to conduct a Sunday school, vacation church school, etc.

1. *The Christian home.*—Only brief comments will here be devoted to the Christian home, in view of its full discussion in Chapter V. The new emphasis on the place of the home in Christian education raises acutely the question of the interrelation of the home and the church. Even if the home should reach the highest efficiency as a teacher of religion, there would still be no lessening of need for the local church to utilize to the full its other agencies for Christian nurture, for the following reasons: (1) The church is the mediator of the Christian faith to the home and must guide the home in the performance of its work of Christian nurture; (2) there are homes represented in the church which are not Christian, or which are otherwise incapable of giving Christian nurture; (3) the task of Christian teaching is great enough to require the wholehearted effort of both church and home; and (4) however effective home teaching may be, its members, young and old, need the fellowship and the training that come from learning the Christian way of life in a larger social group. It is not the home *or* the church as primary teacher, but the home *and* the church as partners in the task.

2. *The Sunday school.*—Traditionally this is *the* agency of Christian education. Others may have value, but the Sunday school is regarded as in a class by itself. The religious education program and the Sunday school are regarded as synonymous expressions. In many churches, the committee on Christian education is expected to concern itself with the Sunday school, and with nothing else.

The historic contribution of the Sunday school should not be minimized. It has given many people their first touch with the church. Many can look back to at least one teacher whose good influence has been indelible. Such Bible knowledge as they possess goes back to Sunday school days. There they learned to worship and to lead in worship. There service projects caught their interest and promoted the spirit of brotherhood. Millions owe to it the chief credit for what growth they have made in Christian living.

Today some are saying that the Sunday school is a declining institution, and predictions are not lacking that it will altogether disappear. They point to a loss of a quarter-million pupils from Protestant Sunday schools in a two-year period, from 1943 to 1945, in face of an increasing general population. Such losses, however, can easily be exaggerated in importance. They can be evaluated only in comparison with losses or gains in population *of the same ages* as those which predominantly make up our Sunday schools. The proportion of children of these ages in our population has also been declining as shown by public school statistics.[1] It is likely that as the proportion of children to the total

[1]These statements are supported by statistics included in the Study Committee report on which this chapter is based.

population begins to rise, Sunday school statistics will show a corresponding increase. Moreover, churches are reaching many by other agencies than the Sunday school and are giving much more time to almost all their pupils than was the case when there were Sunday schools only. Nevertheless, there is a great unreached body of people to which the church should minister with Christian education, and until they are more adequately reached there is no convincing answer to be made to the statistical critics. In this connection it is encouraging to notice the new seriousness with which denominations and interchurch agencies are reaching those hitherto untouched by Christian teaching. Substantial gains have already been achieved by such programs.

Others are attacking the Sunday school on the grounds of the inadequacy of its work. Much of this criticism is justified. If in practice it teaches irreverence or fails to teach the Bible, as is often the case, it has become a liability and not an asset. If it operates with little planning, untrained and irresponsible leadership, and with such haphazard methods that no constructive outcome is possible, then its justification for existence may well be questioned.

It is to the remedy of such deficiencies that this study has been directed. They are not inherent weaknesses of Christian education. They are rather the result of lack of planning, slovenly performance of accepted duties, and disinterest on the part of ministers as well as laymen in this important phase of the church's work. There are so many churches operating on an entirely different basis and in a goodly measure realizing their Christian education objectives that we have grounds for taking courage.

The Sunday school which operates parallel to the church, is independent of the church, and often serves a constituency which has little relation to the church, is obsolete and should be replaced by something more effective. But the idea of including the teaching of religion in a Sunday morning program, in relation to the church, is sound and will remain. New ways of using this time should be adopted as their effectiveness is proved. We are not interested in preserving traditional patterns; we are tremendously concerned with providing the best possible Christian education of which the church is capable.

The Sunday morning program of Christian education will take its place in the total pattern of the church. Organizationally, it will become subordinate to the board of Christian education or other central planning body. The lay superintendent will function under the supervision of this board and, to an extent, as its executive officer, so far as Sunday morning activities are concerned. Other agencies will be employed to render those services which they are peculiarly fitted to perform. This leaves the Sunday morning program free for those things which it can best do, without seeking to carry a complete program. Among the things which can perhaps best be given on Sunday morning are these: systematic study and instruction, with classrooms, competent teachers, good lesson materials, adequate pupil preparation; training and experience in worship; experiences in church life; appeal to the entire church constituency; widest contact with the lay leadership of the church.

3. *The young people's society.*—Churches are concerned about their young people. It is accepted by most of them that there should be a young people's organiza-

tion—several of them in the larger churches—usually holding its meetings on Sunday evening. Apologies are made for its absence when it does not exist. It is customary in church statistics to include a report on the membership of the youth organization.

We have traced the rise and development of youth work in Chapter I. There we saw the purposes which were sought through youth organizations. Many Christians today can testify to the value of youth work in their own lives. With many it has served to bring them into the church, led them to commit their lives to Christ and the church, and opened up for them avenues for Christian service. Even when due allowance is made for the many instances where youth programs have lacked vigor and depth, credit must be given this movement for a tremendous contribution to the life and work of the church.

There have been weaknesses, of course, in youth work. One of them is the tendency to regard itself as a separate entity, not effectively related to the church. Attendance at youth meetings may easily be regarded as a sufficient contact with the church and its work. A wholesome emphasis on self-direction and pupil leadership has often gone so far as to produce this unwholesome result.

A counterpart to this weakness is the tendency on the part of the church to separate itself from its young people. Having made provision for them with an organization and allowed them the use of a part of the building and equipment, the church has often felt that its duty was done. It was expected that in due time these young people would grow into the church. This may not happen automatically. Young people need the more mature guidance which the adults of the church can give them. They need the sense of fellowship which comes from more intimate contact with the whole church.

A third weakness may be found in the programs of youth groups. They may overlap with what is done for the same people elsewhere. They may run heavily to recreational interests. Often they are haphazard, insipid, and unworthy of the church they represent. National organizations have done a noteworthy service in supplying topics and program suggestions. But these helps are of little value when local leaders and youth committees are unwilling to pay the price of making them the expression of their own needs.

These weaknesses are not inherent in youth work but are the result of inadequate leadership and lack of integration. The remedy for them lies in a comprehensive, well-organized program of Christian education for the church, in which youth work takes its place and renders its own peculiar contributions. This process is already well under way in many churches. It calls for a fellowship of all the youth of the church, under the general guidance of the board of Christian education, with youth represented on this board and its committee on youth work. The mere forming of a youth fellowship does not, of course, guarantee effectiveness of program, any more than its absence necessarily means poor work. But it makes more effective work possible. When youth work is planned in this comprehensive fashion, the traditional young people's society is enabled to make the contributions which it is best fitted to render. These include:

a) An opportunity for self-determination in organization and program, under the counsel of competent adult advisers and in the framework of the church.

b) Flexibility in organization and program, with no traditional patterns to which they must adhere. With more time than is usually available in the Sunday school class, more adequate equipment, and no required courses to be covered, the youth group lends itself peculiarly to the discussion and investigation type of program. This has made it appropriate for the youth group to carry those phases of the curriculum which deal with lifework, social issues, love and marriage, and various personal problems. The outcome of this more informal type of program has often led to opportunities for personal counseling.

c) Pupil participation in leadership has been an important factor in leadership training. This was one of the original ideals of the youth movement and continues to be one of its strong features.

d) A strong denominational fellowship bond and, at the same time, an equally strong sense of interdenominational fellowship, reflects one of the interesting trends in youth work. This expresses itself in the pattern of the United Christian Youth Movement and of state youth councils, paralleling a new consciousness of denominational fellowship on national, state, and district or association lines. This trend in youth work is a counterpart of a similar trend in the church as a whole. If young people are to take their place in the life of their denomination and in the cooperative life of Protestantism later on, they must learn to do so by the way of experience.

4. *The vacation church school.*—For half a century the vacation church school has been demonstrating its value. It has gradually been making its way into the regular programs of the churches. The time has come when it should no longer be thought of as an "extra," which a

church may or may not use. The burden of proof should be on every church to show why it does not have one, just as is now the case with the Sunday school and the young people's society.

In too many cases the vacation church school is still an orphan, comparatively unrelated to the church. It should be adopted as a full member in the Christian education family and treated as such. It then becomes one of the opportunities through which the board of Christian education of the church seeks to meet the needs of the people of the parish. This will make it possible to assign to the vacation school the doing of those things which it is best qualified to do.

On page 37 the specific contributions of this agency were presented. They include: (1) more time for Christian education; (2) ample opportunity for such activities as projects, field trips, dramatics, Bible geography, map making, hymn study, study of the church and other churches, exploration of the revelation of God in nature. If some of these can best be done on summer weekdays, the time of the Sunday school need not be occupied with them, thus leaving its workers free for those things which the Sunday morning program can best accomplish.

If its full value is to be realized, certain conditions must be provided for the vacation church school, including at least the following:

a) Its curriculum must be planned as a part of the total church curriculum, and on a long-term basis.

b) It must be held for an adequate term of weeks. A one-week or a two-week school will be helpful, and is certainly better than no vacation school at all. But a five or six weeks' term is necessary if the values we have ascribed to it are to be achieved by the vacation church school. The tendency of so many churches to conduct their Christian education at a minimum level to satisfy conscience should be resisted—for some consciences are too easy to satisfy.

c) A really competent staff of workers must be in charge. Considering the high grade of ability required, the specific training which must be taken, and the amount of time required, it will usually be necessary to include an item in the budget for the compensation of these workers.

d) The budget for the vacation church school should be a part of the budget for Christian education of the church, so as to assure adequate and consistent financing of the school.

e) The minister should use this opportunity to have a vital relation to the children of the church. There are contributions which he can make better than any other person.

f) In cases where several churches cooperate in holding a vacation church school, the opportunity for helping all the children to get a friendly acquaintance with these several churches should not be overlooked.

5. *The weekday church school.*—There are two aspects to the local church's relation to the weekday church school:

a) Each church must utilize what is done in the weekday church school as a part of its own total program. In many churches the board of Christian education does not even know which of the children of the church are enrolled in weekday classes, to say nothing of what they are doing there. The committee must take into account what the weekday school is doing in order to include it in its own total plan; it must acquaint the teachers in the church school with the other Christian education activities in which their pupils are engaged and include the information about the total Christian education experience of the child in his educational records. Local church curricula often can and must be modified to take advantage of what the weekday school is offering.

b) Each church should take its share in the planning and financing of the weekday program. Only thus can it become a part of the Christian education program of all the churches of the community.

In communities where there is more than one Protestant church, weekday classes are usually held on a cooperative basis. Experience has proved this to be the best practice. When there are Catholic churches and Jewish synagogues in the community, the Protestant churches must in turn cooperate with those of the other faiths.

The weekday program should be so worked out that there is the largest possible measure of integration with the local church programs. This is not easy, in view of the wide differences between curricula in the several churches. It remains for the churches in some pioneering community to work out a community-wide plan through which the Sunday, vacation, and weekday curricula of all the churches are so built as to make for maximum integration.

The weekday church school setting is such as to suggest that its contribution to the total Christian education of the child may best be of the instructional-study type. Usually the classes are fairly large, the classrooms and equipment reasonably adequate, textbooks fairly good, teachers well trained, and the anticipation of high-grade work should carry over from the public school from which the pupils have just been released. It would seem, therefore, that the weekday school might major in the study of the Bible, church history, the place of religion in citizenship, the expressions of religion in community life, interfaith and intercultural studies.

Weekday church school work is not always done on as high a plane as the preceding paragraph suggests. That is why all the churches should have the opportunity to make it as effective as possible. It is only by its demonstrated merit that the weekday church school will continue to commend itself to the public school authorities and the community.

In communities where a new venture in weekday religious education is contemplated, the churches through their committees on Christian education should share in the careful and prolonged planning necessary to establish them on a sound basis. The right kind of planning includes proper clearance with those of other faiths, setting up a Protestant organization which is adequate, educating the people of the churches, financing, providing buildings and equipment, selecting curricula, selecting and training teachers, making administrative arrangements with the public school authorities, giving adequate publicity. All this preparatory work will take no less than a year.

There are those who feel that the weekday church school is not an adequate solution to the problem of religion in American education. They insist that to be effective, religious education must be an integral part of the curriculum of the public school. This point of view will be considered in Chapter VII.

6. *Young adult groups.*—During the past decade there has been a growing interest in young adults. The church has been driven to give special attention to them because it has been losing them so tragically. The greatest drop from active church life has come in the period of the twenties. A new strategy is needed to hold this important group in active participation. Having outgrown the comparative limitations of youth, yet with the spirit of pioneering adventure still in them, the young adults might be the very center of new life and growth in any church.

Young adults need the continuing ministry of the church. This is the time of life for new experiences: entrance upon business and profession, homemaking, having children, acquiring property, the assumption of civic responsibilities. How important that religion have a vital part in all of this! The patterns and ideals for life are in process of crystallization during this period.

The program of Christian education of the church can never be regarded as adequate or complete until it includes the young adults. In response to this challenge, thousands of young adult groups have been organized all over the country. There have been few attempts to standardize the organization or program. Perhaps this should never be done, for there is room here for creative new patterns. A large measure of self-direction is possible and desirable with this age group.

From the standpoint of its interest in persons, the church may well allow the young adults to develop their own programs so as to meet their needs for fellowship, instruction, and recreation. From the standpoint of developing the fellowship of Christians, worshiping and serving God through the various activities of the church, it may well look to the young adults to play an important and creative part.

7. *Adult organizations.*—How seldom are adult agencies thought of as having any relations to the educational program of the church! Learning is for children or for adolescents, people think!

But men and women have needs of their own, as great as they have ever had in their lives. The conviction is growing that the most important emphasis in Christian education today is at the adult level. Ours is largely an adult world, whose policies are fixed by the more mature; and those who are more mature are setting the standards and creating the behavior patterns in home and church and community. At a time when society in general is stressing adult education the church must not lag behind. Although we give lip service to the doctrine that adult education is basic we continue to organize our local churches, our denominational agencies, and our interdenominational work as though it were of secondary importance.

Each separate group in the church is potentially a teaching agency. Even though they bear no such name, and even though they have not been organized with this as an objective, they do have educational possibilities. Elected church officers come in this category, for their responsibilities may be made the occasion of careful training and real growth. The same is true of church committees, whose work may be lifted out of the routine and made the occasion of personal growth, deeper insights, and better understanding of the area of their responsibilities. Thus the ongoing, organized work of the church is far more than machinery; it may be merely that, but sometimes, fortunately, it is a learning opportunity; far more often it *could* be a learning opportunity for men and women.

Probably the chief agency of adult education in the average church is the Sunday morning service. The sermon, the Bible reading, and other elements of worship represent the major amount of Christian education for most men and women. This is essential. But more is needed.

Almost all churches have adult organizations. There may be the Men's Brotherhood, the Women's Missionary Society, the Ladies' Aid, the Women's Guild, the Men's Bible Class, the Couples' Club. Each may fulfill some particular function; but at the same time all must avoid the dangers of tradition, exclusiveness, inadequacy of program, and overemphasis on organization, which so easily beset them.

A decade ago the United Christian Adult Movement was launched, with emphasis on worship, study, and action in such areas of life as: the Bible, personal faith and experience, Christian family life, church life and outreach, community issues, social problems, world relations.[2] The church that makes its starting point, not existing organizations, but men and women, will find here fruitful fields for thought. Are the men and women learning, growing, worshiping, achieving, persons? Do they have opportunities along these lines? Are there adult study groups on significant themes? There are opportunities for group worship; is there guidance for individual worship? Are there opportunities for individual and group action toward a more Christian

---

[2]See *Learning for Life*, a pamphlet which outlines a guided study program in these areas. Your denominational publisher or the International Council of Religious Education, 203 North Wabash Ave., Chicago; 15 cents.

society? The important question is: Do the adult organizations of the church believe that they have an *educational* function? Is their program educationally significant? Does the church so plan for its men and women that they are encouraged to participate—and actually do participate—in study groups on religious themes and in other educational opportunities? Is there really an *educational* approach toward postwar planning, toward the relations between Christians and Jews, toward problems of the Christian home?

Society is so organized that men and women may always work in separate groups to a certain extent. But the separation is often carried too far. Side by side they worship in the Sunday morning service. Why should they not be together also in a week-night study class? Why not face, together, some social issue that calls for intelligent action? Whatever advance is made in women's work and in men's work, we need a new advance in adult Christian education, with men and women *together* at study, at worship, and in action.

8. *Preparation for church membership.*—Since we are dealing chiefly with "agencies," this section might have been entitled, "The Pastor's Class." To have done so, however, would have been to miss the point. Training for church membership includes much more than can ever be included in a pastor's Lenten class for young people who anticipate becoming members of the church. Preparation for church membership is an adjustment to the whole life of the church. It is a person's whole experience up to the point of church membership. It includes the religious curriculum that is planned for him, the guided experiences through which he is led, in church and home as well. The pastor's class frequently (not

always) deals with matters of doctrine and beliefs. While it is quite fitting that this instruction should receive particular attention at this very time, it is shortsighted to suppose that this experience—sometimes as brief as an hour a week for six weeks or so—constitutes a satisfactory "preparation" for church membership.

Many a pastor who plans with utmost care for his church membership course concerns himself not at all about the church school curriculum during the six or eight preceding years. He may not be aware that texts are being used that are quite out of harmony with the viewpoint of the church. He needs to realize that the "preparation" for church membership began years before the first session of his class.

Preparation for church membership, therefore, deals with such questions as the Christian home, the church school curriculum, Christian beliefs, service activities of boys and girls, their training experiences in worship, which, for many, culminate with intelligent participation in the sacrament of Holy Communion. People must be trained in worship "to quicken the conscience by the holiness of God, . . . to purge the imagination by the beauty of God, to open the heart to the love of God, to devote the will to the purpose of God."[3]

They must learn what the Christian church essentially is—not a club, a charity, a group which lays down rules to keep people straight, a building, but a *divine redemptive fellowship*. All definitions of the church are inadequate. But clearly one who is trained for church membership has reached a reasonably satisfactory idea of what the church is. The church is truly called catholic,

[3] William Temple. *The Hope of a New World*, p. 30. Macmillan Co., 1943. Used by permission.

in the sense that it is universal in its scope and purpose. The church is the supranational fellowship. It asserts always that "every man is a child of God and as such has a dignity and status independent of his membership in any state." The church is a supraracial fellowship. No matter what their color, God has no favorites among the races. The church is a supraclass fellowship. God makes no social distinctions. The church is the eternal fellowship. One who is "prepared" for church membership must be growing toward such a conception of the church.

When we have grounded people in some better understanding of the church's nature we must not be afraid to encourage healthy criticism of her past and present weaknesses, for the world will pay little heed to the church if it fails to give convincing evidence that it has the power to correct its own defects.

Preparation for church membership goes farther than up to the time of the act itself. After that has taken place the whole life and program of the church must be an experience in churchmanship. One church has a program described as "completing the act of church membership"—a series of classes or learning experiences designed to bring the new member (young or old) into a real understanding of the work and purpose of the local church, the denomination, and the Christian church in its widest outreach. Training in churchmanship does not stop with the act of membership. It continues, through worship and participation in the work of the church, through fellowship in the outreach of the church, and through continued learning (even for men and women) in the various areas of the church's life and task.

9. *Choirs.*—Choirs are an opportunity for a twofold ministry: (1) the ministry that the choir renders to the people of the congregation, and (2) the ministry that the experience itself renders to the members of the choir. If the task is merely a professional one, with the motive of money or recognition rather than of service, the major values are lost.   If the experience is one of Christian training and Christian service, there are values for both participants and hearers that make this an important factor in religious education.   This is why churches often have children's and youth choirs as well as one composed of adults.   If there are values in the experience itself, surely children and young people as well as men and women deserve to share in these values.

What are these values?   Members of children's choirs establish the habit of regular worship attendance, gain knowledge through experience of the principles and practices of Christian worship and a growing acquaintance with the rich heritage of Christian hymns, anthems, and sacred music.   They come to know the great passages of the Bible through the most perfect emotional channel, music.   Children's and young people's choirs become excellent training grounds for senior choirs.   Their participation in the worship service is an inspiration to the whole congregation, symbolizing the ongoing life of Christian fellowship among persons of all ages.

A choir experience is a part of one's experience of Christian nurture, but rarely is it so regarded.   The leader needs to be chosen, not only for his musical ability, but also because he is a religious person, alert to the objectives of Christian education.   This whole field must come more under the purview of the board of Christian education than is usually the case.

10. *Camps and conferences.*—Under this heading are included all such ventures as intermediate camps, young people's camps and conferences, adult camps and conferences, training schools, family camps, summer assemblies, week-end camps, work camps, and caravans.

Camps and conferences are of all types—denominational, interdenominational, and nondenominational. It is a rapidly growing movement which has already reached considerable proportions. It is difficult to get figures on the number of persons participating in camps and conferences every year, but a conservative estimate would place it at several hundred thousand. In the summer of 1943 one denomination, by no means one of the largest Protestant churches, enrolled more than 12,000 persons in its camp and conference program.

The purpose of the camp and conference program is the same as that of the total Christian education program, with emphasis on personal development, training in churchmanship and Christian leadership and service, and recruiting for Christian service. While it has the same broad objective, it is only a small part of that total program and is supplementary to it. It is limited in the number reached in proportion to the total number in the churches but has an influence far out of proportion to the time spent and the numbers reached. Although the program may be similar to that of the home church in many ways, the whole atmosphere and spirit of the summer conference tend to heighten its effectiveness and to make it one of the most significant experiences of the year.

The cumulative effect of a week or two weeks spent in camp with all the waking hours carefully planned to render the maximum Christian influence often proves to be one of the formative experiences for young people. It is possible that the camp and conference program which has grown with such amazing speed in the last quarter century will prove to be as powerful an agency of Christian education in our day as the Sunday school came to be in another generation.

This camp and conference program has ministered largely to young people between the ages of twelve and twenty-four, with emphasis on the older group, from about sixteen to twenty-four (chiefly the 15-18 age range). But in recent years there has been a rapid growth in the number of camps for the younger group from twelve to fourteen. There are also adult conferences enrolling a considerable number.

The emphasis in many adult conferences has been on leadership training, and they have usually been held in the more formal atmosphere of a campus, with the curriculum correspondingly formal. But there are now many adult camps and conferences of the enrichment type, built on the needs of men and women themselves, rather than on their responsibilities as leaders.

The camp and conference movement has so proved its value that it is clear that such experiences in Christian education should be made available to many more people, young and older. This will probably require a trend in the direction of making such opportunities more readily available to local communities. Many more local churches should have camps of their own. Councils of churches could render a distinct service by making camp sites available for the use of individual churches or groups of churches working together.

The local church will consider the camp and conference as a part of its total program of Christian education and plan wisely for the participation of its people in such enterprises. Also it will be alert to take advantage of the new enthusiasm, knowledge, and skills with which its people return from the camp and conference for more effective service in the church.

11. *Pastoral ministry.*—The personal service of the minister, and to some extent of lay workers, is an important part of the service of the church to individuals and families. While such ministry may not be primarily educational in purpose, it has vast possibilities for guiding growth in Christian faith and life. In these personal contacts the minister has an opportunity to see the whole person in his individual needs and to guide him as his needs indicate. This intimate understanding of the people of the parish should influence program planning at many points, and this is another indication that the minister needs to be closely related to these planning activities.

V. The Experimental Attitude

This study of the organization of the church for Christian education, and of the agencies through which it is carried on, necessarily leaves many questions and problems untouched.

It has not been possible to include a consideration of the important matter of educational records. Surely this new conception of total program will require some re-examination of record systems and the way in which records are kept.

It has not been possible to deal with the important ministry of the church to families with children that are too young to be in the church school ("Cradle Roll"). Neither has it been possible to deal with the church's outreach to those who by sickness or other deterring circumstance are prevented from attending its services ("Home Department").

It has not been possible, except by implication, to deal with the urgent problem of reaching the unchurched. Providing a good quality of program for those already in the constituency is of course of primary importance. But may not the extension of the church's educational service to the unreached go on parallel with it? This phase has been neglected in recent years. Some of the new patterns such as the vacation and weekday schools have served to reach many new children, but churches have been slow to follow up these opportunities. The new emphasis on the whole family is in the right direction. But more needs to be done. The present mobility of the American population has greatly increased the problem. Canvasses and personal visitation campaigns, follow-up of absentees, welcome to new families, utilization of contacts through Christian ministry to families, are but a few among scores of ways of reaching the unchurched. The dynamic of evangelism is more important than techniques, and the church which has the warm evangelistic spirit among its members will find ways that are effective.

In conclusion, we would urge that each church assume an experimental attitude and be alert to ways in which it may creatively develop its own program. There is no evidence that any particular agency for Christian education is the best. In some churches the Sunday school is the most effective, in others the youth group, in still others the vacation church school. Moreover, there has been enough experimentation with new patterns of accomplishing the old purposes to make us hesitate to defend any particular agency because of its long history or because of what it may have done for any particular individual. These new patterns include such things as the camping movement, the junior church, education by radio, direct service to family groups in the home, neighborhood groups, various types of activities for young adults, and many others. The point of importance seems to be that the objective of Christian education must be clearly conceived and the means used for its achievement that are most appropriate to any particular situation. It sometimes happens that the old things can best be done in new ways because new ways draw new enthusiasms to them.

There will no doubt be some who say that we have been too conservative in our suggestions. They are convinced that present programs for Christian education are not successful and that something entirely new must be found. With some this takes the form of calling for the abandonment of lay leadership and putting Christian teaching in the hands of those who are properly trained and adequately paid to give the necessary time. Others feel that the Sunday school is utterly hopeless and that religion should properly be put back into the curriculum of the public school.

To all such, we can only answer that (1) we are painfully aware of the inadequacies of present-day Christian education; (2) we are just as anxious as they to see it much more effective; (3) we believe that the application of drastic new patterns and methods awaits a change of heart on the part of most families and churches; (4) we think that existing patterns and agencies may become very effective, once such change of heart has taken place and they are adequately used; and (5) let those who would see the problem approached more radically proceed to experiment with their ideas, for new patterns are not born by national pronouncement but by local initiative.

Chapter IV

The Curriculum of Christian Education

*T*HROUGHOUT the preceding chapters we have assumed an organized program of Christian education for the church. We must now consider more specifically what that program is. The word "curriculum" is used as a name for an educational program.

I. THE MEANING OF CURRICULUM

In the broadest sense of the term, all life is the curriculum. There is no experience which does not have an influence on what people become. And if religion is concerned with all phases of life, then most of life's experiences may be thought of as the religious curriculum. This conception would include: the temper and life of the home, the life of the church, the life of the environing community with all its tributary institutions, and every last significant contact which the individual makes —all these constitute the curriculum of *his* Christian education. The distinguishing feature of this conception of curriculum is that it sees the individual as a whole, in all his contacts, and recognizes the outcome in his character as the result of all these forces.

This conception of curriculum is too broad for practical purposes. That all these forces are important in growth and development cannot be denied. Indeed, it is because they have so often not been taken into account by the church that Christian education has been comparatively ineffective. But we need a conception of curriculum which gives a church board of Christian education something tangible to work with.

A second way in which the curriculum of Christian education is defined has it include all those activities and experiences which are initiated or utilized by the church for the achievement of the aims of Christian education. These activities and experiences will include things done for the pupils, activities which the pupils themselves are led into doing, environing conditions which influence thought and attitudes, persons with whom the pupils come in contact, fellowship groups in which they are immersed, books and other source materials, and their life situations and problems outside the church which are used as illustrations of Christian living and the setting for Christian conduct. The distinguishing feature of this conception of curriculum is that it embraces the conscious efforts of the leaders in the church to help its pupils to put their entire lives under the guidance and control of the Christian gospel.

There is yet a third conception of curriculum. This limits the term to the prepared materials for use in the church's program of Christian education. This includes books for teachers and pupils, periodicals, pictures, hymns and music, slides and motion pictures. The term "lesson materials" is often used to describe these printed materials. The distinguishing feature of this conception is that it views curriculum from the standpoint of what may be done for the local church by some outside group to cause it to have an effective program.

The second conception recognizes this third in that it usually makes large use of such materials and finds in them its guidance for its own program. The third recognizes the second in that it knows that printed materials are sterile until they come to life within the educational program of a local church. We consider the second definition the most useful. This discussion will, however, give considerable attention to the third approach because good lesson materials are so important in most churches as a basis for their curriculum development.

II. THE PRESENT CURRICULUM SITUATION

It is now three-quarters of a century since systematic provision was made for the curriculum of the Sunday school in the form of Uniform Lessons, and this historic event was itself preceded by almost fifty years of more sporadic effort at lesson making. During that time a bewildering variety of materials has been put forward for the program of Christian education in its several parts and agencies.

1. *Types of materials now available.*—At the present time, the following major types of curriculum materials are available to the churches:

a) Uniform lessons. These materials, designed for and used in the Sunday school almost exclusively, provide essentially the same lesson on any given Sunday for children, youth, and adults alike. There is diversity of treatment and even of emphasis from one age to another; but the same biblical passage, be it large or small, serves as the starting point for all alike. In this sense, they are uniform.

b) Group graded lessons (also called "departmental graded" and "cycle graded"). These materials, also intended primarily for the Sunday school, group the pupils into departments, with a typical age span of three years. On any given Sunday all the pupils of one department, such as the primary, have the same lesson, while the pupils in the junior, junior high school, or other departments each have different lessons.

c) Closely graded lessons. Here the principle of gradation is carried one step further, and a separate course of lessons is provided for each year as in the case of the public school curriculum. These materials, too, are designed primarily for the Sunday school.

d) Elective courses. Some denominational and independent publishers offer a considerable number of separate study units, which may be elected at will by a church or a group in a church. Each one undertakes to cover one definite field of study and is aimed at one age group. They appear either in pamphlet or in book form.

e) Vacation school texts. These materials are typically in book form, are usually provided for the teacher alone, and follow the departmental principle of grading.

f) Weekday school texts. These, too, are typically in book form, are provided in some cases for the teacher alone, in others for both teachers and pupils, and cover an age span of one, two, or three years.

g) Youth fellowship or society topics. The materials offered under this heading are difficult to describe or classify. Many are released weekly in youth magazines. At the opposite extreme, some assume the form of a book or manual containing program suggestions for an entire year.

The foregoing enumeration is by no means complete. It makes no mention of the curricular offerings for men's and women's groups in the church, pastors' classes, missionary organizations, or the guidance of religious growth in the home. It does attempt to set down the chief types of materials which have been developed within the Christian education movement and program in the past and are being used in the present.

2. *Encouraging developments.*—Four encouraging aspects in the present curriculum situation may be noted.

a) There have been constant and marked improvements in such materials—in appearance, gradation, and educational content. The paper used is usually of good quality; the type is suitable for easy reading and adapted to the age of the pupil; pictures and other illustrations are being more attractively reproduced; and there is sometimes a judicious use of color and white space. However, these are trends only, and there is still a long way to go if such materials are to catch up with what these same pupils are reading at home and in school.

A like improvement of substantial degree has been made at the point of adaptation of material to the age of the learner. The language used comes much closer to the idiom of childhood, youth, or adulthood, as the case may be. The verbal and pictorial illustrations also come much closer home.

On a deeper level still, a like improvement is to be noted at the point of the relevancy of curricular materials to the ongoing lives of the learners. Not only are the type and language better suited to the age in question than they used to be, but, even more fundamentally, this is true of the lesson topic and its unfolding. We have become increasingly sensitized to the actual daily life situations in which boys and girls, men and women, find themselves and have slanted our curricular materials toward the places where they truly live.

b) There is an increasing use of suitable supplemental materials. This may take the form of books, large colored pictures, periodicals, slides, motion pictures and other visual aids, hymns and music, and the resources in the church and the community.

c) There has been very real cooperation among Protestant denominations in the curriculum field. This is most marked in the production of lesson outlines but has extended considerably to lesson production also. The problems of cooperation in publication are difficult. Each denomination has developed its own editorial and publishing services to meet best the needs of its constituency. To coordinate these several interests to function as a unit, and in the interest of all of Protestantism, is no small task. Yet, more progress along this line must be made. The churches could benefit in terms of lower prices and better quality if the duplications now existing in Protestant publication could be eliminated. United action at the point of the editorial and publishing functions could greatly increase the quality and variety of Christian education materials of Protestantism without increasing the cost to local churches. Fortunately the present trend is strongly in the direction of cooperative publication. The Missionary Education Movement, with its theme cooperatively selected for each year, and its graded texts attractively produced for the use of all, is an example of what cooperative effort can accomplish.

d) The place of the home in any curriculum of Christian education is increasingly recognized. We ought never to have left it out of consideration; it is at least encouraging that we are coming back to it.

3. *Persistent problems.*—The field of curriculum production presents a number of vexing problems, five of which will be briefly described here:

a) There is confusion in curriculum theory. Two points of view have been struggling for mastery. One of these is the so-called content-centered view, which regards "material to be taught" as the heart of the curriculum. The other is the so-called life-situation point of view, which regards the ongoing experience of the pupil as the heart of the curriculum. Neither of these has won out over the other, nor has a satisfactory synthesis of the two been achieved. Worse still, much present-day lesson making proceeds as though there were no conflict in theory, to the confusion of the users of such lessons.

In the initial curriculum efforts, the first of these tendencies held the field. Present-day Uniform Lessons are the lineal descendents of these material-centered lessons, although a measure of the life-situation principle has been introduced even into them. In the last quarter century, the so-called "creative" or "progressive" theory in education has been making its impact on the church school field, and heroic efforts have been made in the graded lessons, the vacation and weekday texts, the youth programs, and some of the elective courses to carry this theory into practice. These efforts have often been unsuccessful, due to a lack of understanding of this new type of materials by the local church workers. This and a renewed emphasis in Protestantism on the Bible and the content of the Christian faith have again sharply raised this issue of the organizing principle for the curriculum of Christian education. This problem will be given further attention in the next section of this chapter.

b) Churches have been slow to accept and use what curriculum makers have regarded as the higher types of materials. The popularity of the Uniform Lessons constitutes evidence to this effect. There are some churches which use Uniform Lessons after due consideration because they consider them best to meet their needs. Though they may be mistaken, it is right for them to make such selection if they have honestly and intelligently come to this conviction. Most others probably use Uniform Lessons because of tradition, or of following the line of least resistance, or in reaction away from the more progressive types of materials. Most denominational curriculum committees, editors, and publishers would like to go much further into educationally adequate materials than their churches will let them.

c) There is poor use made of the materials furnished to the local church. Prepared curricula are quite generally used in a conventional and stereotyped manner, many steps removed from the curriculum maker's ideal of how they should develop in the warm life of a vigorous local group. All too many leaders "teach the quarterly," instead of using it as an aid in teaching living and growing persons.

The fault lies partly with the local churches and their leaders. They have inadequately faced the problem of what constitutes a curriculum in the local church and the relation of printed material to it. There has been too little effort to understand and use printed materials as they were intended to be used. Too little effort has been devoted to the training and supervision of workers.

But the difficulty is also partly inherent in what is attempted. When the purpose of the educational process is to teach some body of knowledge, it is not hard to set out in a textbook the content and a plan for teaching it. But when the purpose is that of developing a creative experience in a learning group, there are distinct limits to what can be done through a textbook. Such a curriculum must develop in the local setting. Textbooks may give suggestions but they cannot successfully give rules of procedure. Until the local workers master the meaning and method of such program development in the groups they are leading, there is little chance for a creative curriculum, no matter how good the textbooks. Once teachers have grasped this meaning and method, they are comparatively independent of manuals of procedure. There seem to be distinctive limits, therefore, to what can be done by way of curriculum development apart from the local group.

d) There is a multiplicity of agencies through which Christian education is carried on in the local church. We have previously described these agencies and suggested the distinctive contribution which each might render. We have insisted that the program for the local church should be one unified whole. Yet, as we have seen earlier in this chapter, the curricula now available are still largely planned for the Sunday school, the vacation school, and other such agencies, with little relation to each other.

The problem is enormously increased by the fact that these agencies exist in varying numbers in any church and that the pupils in any church school participate in them in varying degrees. If there is a central core of curriculum for Christian education, this ought to be assigned to that agency which deals most effectively with the largest number. But who would undertake to name that agency which consistently meets these qualifications in all churches?

Efforts at unified planning have not been lacking. In 1922 the International Sunday School Lesson Committee appointed a subcommittee charged with the task "to undertake the construction of a curriculum of religious education which shall provide in integrated fashion for both Sunday and weekday hours.'' That worthy effort resulted only in a ''Curriculum Guide'' for curriculum makers, and not in materials for the local church. Current efforts in the lesson committees of the International Council of Religious Education are again looking toward the production of lesson outlines which will make possible the production of a comprehensive curriculum. We await with interest the results of these efforts.

In the final analysis, it is the problem of the local church to make a unified curriculum a reality. In so far as the weekday church school is included, the problem becomes an interchurch one for any given community. But published curriculum materials should help this local effort, not hinder it.

e) How may the home in actual fact be made a part of a total curriculum of Christian education? Certainly the need for doing so is now clearly recognized. But the way to bring about this desired result is still to be found. This problem will be dealt with more fully in the next chapter.

There is, however, one aspect of the problem of home-church relationship which should be dealt with here. This concerns the home's cooperation in the work of the church school. Parental ignorance and indifference are in the forefront of deterring factors in developing an effective church program. It is folly to assume that effective Christian education can be carried on in the time usually available to the church, or under the general ''don't care'' attitude of pupils. Since it seems impossible in most churches to get an adequate block of time so that supervised study may be carried on in the church, it must be expected that those pupils who are old enough to pursue systematic studies will supplement the church time with home study. This requires parental cooperation.

III. A THEORY OF THE CURRICULUM

The basic assumptions of Christian education are the foundation of the curriculum. A statement of the implications of these assumptions for the curriculum constitutes the theory of the curriculum. Chapter II of this book contains the basic assumptions on which we are proceeding, and it remains but to state what they mean in terms of the curriculum of Christian education.

Let no one think that this will be easy. Since at many points there is disagreement on the full implications of the basic assumptions, there will be disagreements as to curriculum theory. Moreover, the solution does not lie in making a statement so broad as to comprehend all points of view. That will lead to confusion. Yet there must be a way of stating a theory of the curriculum which will be generally satisfactory and which will take account of most of the fundamental assumptions on which we are working.

In any case, the attempt must be made. Curriculum construction, either in a national denominational board or in a local church board of Christian education, cannot satisfactorily proceed without some agreement on the underlying assumptions. If an effective learning process is to be developed, the curriculum makers and curriculum users must have a mutual understanding of the underlying theory on which they are working.

The crucial question in curriculum theory may be stated as follows: What shall be the *organizing principle* of the curriculum? The answers which have been made to this question fall into two general groups. The first finds the organizing principle in acquainting the learner with and adjusting him to some part of the heritage and content of the Christian faith. This may be the Bible, the redemptive activity of God in Christ, the major doctrines of the Christian faith, the church year. The second finds it in the present life experience of the learner, as an individual and as a member of a group, such as the home, church, community, world.

The problem would not be so difficult if a simple choice of one of these would suffice. But the moment such a choice is contemplated, it is at once clear that the other holds so much of truth that it cannot be left out. Either point of view, to the exclusion of the other, will not give a satisfactory curriculum. An exclusive use of the first runs into the danger of remoteness from life, fruitless intellectualism, and pedantic authoritarianism. An exclusive use of the second runs into the grave danger of trying to educate without content, in an intellectual and a cultural vacuum, cut off from the rich heritage of the past and the enriching contacts of the present.

We are forced to conclude that any satisfactory theory of curriculum must come out of a synthesis of these two opposing points of view. This is more than merely seeking to reconcile opposites. It is an attempt to see them in proper relation to each other in the light of the needs of persons.

The purpose of the curriculum of Christian education is to confront individuals with the eternal gospel and to nurture within them a life of faith, hope, and love, in keeping with the gospel. The organizing principle of the curriculum, from the viewpoint of the Christian gospel, is to be found in the changing needs and experiences of the individual as these include his relation to (1) God, as revealed in Jesus Christ; (2) his fellow men and human society; (3) his place in the work of the world; (4) the Christian fellowship, the church; (5) the continuous process of history, viewed as a carrier of the divine purpose and revealer of the moral law; (6) the universe in all its wonder and complexity.

A statement in such concise form deserves further elaboration as to its implications. We note, therefore:

1. That this viewpoint turns the spotlight of attention on the individual learning person, for it recognizes that results can be measured only in terms of *his* growth in Christian faith and life. It is *his* experience that must be at the base of his understanding, acceptance, and living of the Christian faith, and *his* problems as a changing individual in a changing world which must be met. It thus conserves the insights which have come from the study of persons and how they learn, which have been associated with "experience-centered" education. These insights are sound and meaningful in the process of Christian education.

2. But it does not view the curriculum as centered in "raw" experience—experience for its own sake, neutral in quality, going nowhere in particular. Rather it pictures the curriculum as taking shape around experience which stands in definitely Christian relations and moves in a definitely Christian direction. To say the same thing differently, it puts at the center of the curriculum, not the individual, per se, but the individual viewed as a Christian disciple. To say it once more, it sees at the center of the curriculum an individual learner, not in splendid isolation, but in vital relation to the great reali-

ties of the Christian faith and life—God, Jesus, fellow men, the Bible, the church, the world. The term "person centered" is thus given a turn which does not thrust these great realities out toward the periphery of the curriculum but brings them in close to the person whose education and salvation are our great concern.

3. The Bible and the total Christian heritage are essential in Christian education. In them we have the record of God's revelation of himself to mankind and of man's response to this revelation. Here we have the sources for an understanding of God's great redemptive purpose, resources in meeting present-day problems, a critique of present practices, and an enrichment to current experience. How can there be Christian education without the Christian gospel?

Clarence Tucker Craig, in the words that follow, has indicated the place which Christian education has in the presentation of the gospel faith:

It is not something we create. The gospel concerns the acts of God. We must first understand it, and then it either awakens belief or unbelief. Christian faith is not the goal of a quest, but a starting point for one. It is not first of all a problem, but a possible answer to life's problems. If one accepts the gospel as true, he must then discover what should follow in practical living. . . .

. . . .

The record of God's revelation to men must be presented as factual material. . . . The most vital need of any person [is] to examine for himself the historic bases of Christian faith. Since Christianity is an historic faith, it cannot be studied through contemporary experiences, but only through the record of God's revelation. Of course, there are other aspects of Christian education.[1]

[1] C. T. Craig, *The Use of the Bible in Teaching*, pp. 6-8 (pamphlet). Board of Education of the Methodist Church, Nashville. Used by permission.

4. Within this theory, a wide variety of approaches to individual curriculum units are made possible. None will move solely on the level of current experience, and none solely on the level of content. Some will be concerned with ongoing life experience, with much use of helpful content. Others will explore, step by step, some body of content, with constant relevancy to life experience. There need be no apology for either approach as long as consistency and balance are maintained in the over-all pattern for the church. We have already suggested that each of the several agencies for Christian education in the church is adapted to a particular type of curriculum work. A unified curriculum plan for the whole church will do more than avoid overlapping of content; it will assure consistency of purpose, proper distribution and sequence of content, and variety of method.

At this point it may be asked, Would a curriculum so conceived be necessarily and inescapably Christian? To make sure that this question may be answered in the affirmative, a Christian master motif should run through all the units of whatever sort. This may be stated as "God's redemptive purpose in Christ to men," to use a phrase of John Mackay. This phrase would not be constantly and tediously reiterated, nor would the ideas be dragged in artificially on each page. Rather, it would be in the foreground of the thinking of all who prepare curriculum materials and of all who teach in the church. From them it would find its way subtly into each unit, giving it a distinctive coloration, a characteristic turn, and orienting it along with all the others toward "the one divine event toward which the whole curriculum moves." Furthermore, this motif must not only be written into printed materials, but must also inform and infuse the life of the local church, the Christian community, which is the necessary context and condition of all Christian education worthy of the name.

A further question may arise, Would such a curriculum have unity, continuity, and cumulative movement toward the high purpose of Christian education? To this end, there may be real advantage in arranging adjacent units into "constellations," which would be cumulative in their movement toward a single objective, despite differences in the nature and content of the several units. For example, a succession of junior high units on the meaning of church membership, the history of the Christian church, the Book of Acts, the missions of the denomination in question, and the Christian answer to the racial problem might all be so handled as to have the net effect of heightening the learners' apprehension of the church as a timeless and boundless fellowship. The accomplishment of such a purpose might require that a single writer prepare the materials for an entire year in order to avoid spottiness and disjointedness. It certainly would require that the materials for the teacher help him to maintain a large perspective, in which the contribution of each part to the whole would be clearly seen and pursued.

IV. Basic Needs Which the Curriculum Must Meet

What should the curriculum of Christian education include? It rests under a profound obligation to answer every honest and legitimate demand made upon it. It is, however, first, last, and always a curriculum of *Christian* education. Within its proper scope, it should be responsive to every need addressed to it from every legitimate source and should be sensitive to register the changes which occur in these needs from time to time and from place to place.

1. *The Christian gospel.*—The first and most insistent call made on the curriculum of Christian education is to be true to the Christian faith. Every portion and every unit of the curriculum should reflect the basic foundations laid down in Chapter II and be true to them. This is a "constant" of the curriculum, which is to be presupposed beneath and behind everything else we say concerning it.

2. *The individual.*—Christian education is concerned with persons, not in isolation, but persons in relation to what has been and what now is. In every age, we look to the curriculum to mediate Christian faith to them, in changing accents, suited to their time, their need, and their perplexities. As we consider the time in which we live, and predict possible trends in the years ahead, we may well consider that the following needs of persons should be given major attention:

a) The need for comfort and security is always present, but particularly so in wartime and in a postwar period. Even though America has been spared the worst ravages of war, there are still thousands, young and old, who have been bereaved, other thousands who have been grossly disillusioned, and yet others who have been uprooted by the war. In the great Christian affirmations, there is comfort for bereavement and hope in times of chaos. In the humble dependency on the moving Spirit of God, there is salvation from disillusionment. In communion with God and the ministry of the Christian church, there is security and fellowship. Now is the time for the curriculum to speak a word of assurance and salvation to distraught souls, with all the ways at its command.

b) The need for some clear moral guidance is peculiarly imperative in our day. War tends to become the negation of all moral values. Our Western civilization has fallen under the spell of a widespread relativism, by which all absolute moral values have been abandoned. We have weighed, analyzed, and examined; we have thought a thing right for one person but not for another; right here but not there; right now but not then. Rarely does moral conviction rise to the imperative, "Thus saith the Lord!" The result is not only moral confusion, but also moral laxity and indifference. The curriculum must give clear guidance in this uncertainty.

c) There is need for a sense of community, undergirded by an understanding and experience of true democracy. The trend of the day is toward deep cleavages in the spirit of community because of interrace and interclass hatreds. Primary social groupings, such as the family and the neighborhood, are being weakened. The possibility of making the world one community comes every day more near, but the forces which crack the world into fragments are too strong to be overcome by the forces of cohesion. Believing that democracy, which aims ultimately at the development of the individual into mature social responsibility, is an expression of the Christian faith, our curriculum must endeavor to interpret it and employ its methods in actual practice.

d) To help people to know what they believe is another fundamental task of the curriculum of Christian education. There is widespread ignorance of things religious due to ineffective teaching, confusion because of the uncertainty with which Christian education has spoken on matters of Christian belief, widespread doubt because of the impact of un-Christian forces on youth today as never before. To teach the Christian verities is always important, but particularly so in a day of such great uncertainty as ours.

e) There is need for vital membership in the Christian fellowship, the church. In the church we have a society within a society, a grouping with its own standards of membership, patterns of life, and heritage from the past. Once the individual can find a sure rootage for his life within this Christian fellowship, he is well on the way to the meeting of many of his other needs.

3. *The home.*—Two considerations indicate the demands of the home on the curriculum. The first is that the home as a basic institution in American life is gravely imperiled. It is losing ground in point of space, in point of time which the members spend there together, in point of numbers in the family, in point of essential services it renders its members, in point of the strength of the hold which it has on its members.

The second is the increasing recognition of the home as the place where Christian nurture will be most effectively carried on. If it fails, nothing which the church can possibly do within its own walls will suffice to compensate for this failure.

Consequently, the home looks to Christian education for help in maintaining its own integrity as a fundamental social institution and help in the performance of its task of Christian nurture. These are curriculum problems. Since they are to be dealt with more fully in the next chapter, they will be left here with the mere statement of them.

4. *The church.*—Fundamentally, the church asks help in arousing its membership fully to the importance of its teaching task, and helping them in accomplishing it. Beyond this, the following specific needs remain to be met:

a) The new emphasis on the ecumenical spirit needs to be reflected in the church's curriculum. Adequate training in church membership should introduce persons into the fellowship of the church universal as well as that of their own denomination. The success of the ecumenical movement tomorrow depends largely on what we write into our curricula today.

b) There is need for renewed emphasis on the church's heritage. Some years ago a study was conducted among four thousand boys and girls in grades four to nine throughout Episcopal Sunday schools of the United States. The investigator found these children inadequately informed concerning the life of the church, unprepared to use the resources of the church well, and imperfectly acquainted with the sacraments and symbols of the church.[2] These results are all the more striking in that they come out of a communion which has long stressed churchmanship. The need, therefore, is great for a more adequate handling within our curriculum of the church's history, the church's great biographies, the church's symbolism, music, art, architecture, worship, and sacraments, and the church's manifold achievements in individual and social life.

c) A new emphasis upon evangelism is needed. There are doubtless many ways in which the recaptured evan-

[2]Frances R. Edwards, *Children and the Church.* Ph.D. thesis at Teachers College, Columbia University, 1935.

gelistic passion of the church will be reflected in curricular materials, of which the following may serve as a starting point: The materials can be so written as to confront each individual of whatever age with the eternal gospel in terms so dynamic and unmistakable as to call for a forthright decision. They can include the type of study and activity units which will give every disciple some actual experience at being an evangelist. And, for the leader, they can offer recurrent suggestions of an inspirational and practical nature calculated to make him restless until he reaches everyone possible with the Christian message and for the Christian fellowship.

5. *The social order.*—The social order in which we live makes a rightful demand on the curriculum of Christian education. It is ill, nigh unto death. The symptoms of its illness may be seen in the unspeakable horrors of war, the inability to attain international understanding which will promote lasting peace, the economic and social chaos following the war and resulting often in the very things which the war was waged to eliminate, and the worldwide apprehension so suddenly engendered by the terrors of atomic power. What may Christian education do in the face of this need?

a) It may give a factual and realistic interpretation to its pupils of the social situation in which they live. They should be given cold, hard facts and equipped with the readiness and ability to supplement, evaluate, and interpret all sources of information. How many children are undernourished and inadequately clothed? How many are denied adequate play space and life in the great out-of-doors in summertime? Where can Negro children go swimming? What are the actual causes of war? What are the prospects for peace? What is the truth about Russia? What dare we expect from the United Nations? What is the truth about wages and hours? Is industry making excessive profits? The answers to these questions are not easy to find, but the habit of looking for facts before coming to conclusions is an important one to establish. How can people project what should be unless they know what is?

b) It may help define the goal for a Christian society, rooted in the eternal will of God. We commonly define this goal in the words "the fatherhood of God and the brotherhood of all men." But what does this mean when brought down to earth? How much power ought labor unions to exercise in a fully Christian society? What place would there be for cooperatives? How much of a range should there be between the highest salary and the lowest wage? Should whites and Negroes live in segregation, but with equal opportunity for all, or in complete social mutuality? In short, what is it in concrete terms that Christians are working and praying for?

c) It may help to discover practical ways in which Christians as individuals and as groups can actually take hold. It is one thing to know what ought to be, but quite another thing to know how to help bring it to pass. Should a congregation as a congregation ever support a given political candidate? With what groups and organizations can a socially conscious individual with a Christian motivation align himself? What are the best ways of actually getting results within a local community? Any curriculum desirous of playing fair with the social order must deal with questions such as these. And, after it has dealt with them, it may well offer wise and tested and compelling suggestions for going beyond mere talking to actual doing. The social problems to be included in the curriculum are legion, and selection may be made in the light of the needs of the times, the community in question, the particular group making the study, and the age of the pupils composing the study group.

6. *The teachers.*—In the final analysis, curriculum comes into actual being at the point where teachers work with groups of pupils. The adequacy of curriculum materials must always be measured in terms of the way in which they come to life in the local group. To meet this rigorous test is not easy, for those who use the prepared material are a very heterogeneous group—old and young, educated and ignorant, skilled and untrained, faithful and careless. Worse still, they are to some extent all mixed up in any church, so that it is not possible to classify churches by their types of workers and give them curricula accordingly. The materials must be so prepared that they will meet the needs of all these types of workers.

a) Such materials must therefore, on the one hand, give explicit instruction in one-two-three order, on how to proceed in making the best use of the time available. These instructions must be simple, unmistakable, reasonable, and practical. On the other hand, there must be flexibility for those workers who are ready to proceed in more creative fashion. It is not easy to combine these two approaches. Nevertheless, the attempt must be made, for the reason that the same material will be used here by an unskilled worker, and there by one possessed of greater resourcefulness. If any sacrifice is to be made, let it be in favor of the former. Perhaps the solution lies in offering a clear, simple teaching procedure as a base, and then supplying additional and alternative suggestions for those equipped to go the second mile.

b) Practical and easy-to-follow guidance in educational method needs to be given, with the emphasis always on method as the means to an end. This applies in particular to the newer methods, such as discussion and project. We scarcely realize how strange these appear to many teachers, reared under a different system. Therefore, our suggestions can scarcely be made too explicit or too full. "This is the way to start. . . . This is what may have to be done next. . . . After this happens, go on from there in this direction."

c) Curriculum materials must help workers with the difficult art of making the curriculum a genuine experience of the local group. The conception that the essence of teaching is the impartation of knowledge is so widespread that most workers need to be given a new outlook. They need help in making a study of their own pupils, through suggestions of feasible ways of observing them, keeping records of observations, and discovering the objectives of teaching in the pupil's own experience and needs. Then they need also to be helped to make a given subject of study "at home" in the local church. No lesson writer can prepare a unit on race relations, for example, to be equally suitable for churches in Boston, or Atlanta, or any other place in the country. Such a unit does not become effective curriculum until it grows out of the race problems of the community where it is taught and, in turn, leads to action with respect to them.

d) In units which require it, there needs to be an adequate presentation of background materials—the Bible, church history, and the like. This should be scholarly, interesting, vital, and satisfying to heart as well as mind. The past must be made to come alive. This is not easy to achieve through the printed page, but it must be done. Every now and then there arises a biblical scholar or a church historian with the necessary dramatic sense to make characters and events of the past rise up and move before us in a living procession. Generally such persons are found to have an unusual combination of scholarship, imagination, and humor. It is precisely this combination, plus sound educational training, which is needed for the preparation of curricular materials.

e) Lesson materials themselves cannot contain all the guidance which an enterprising teacher will need. This requires that reference be made to other resources. These may include books, Bible dictionaries and encyclopedias, pictures, magazines, visual aids, and the like. Too formidable a list may serve only to appall or aggravate the average leader. The references chosen should be nontechnical, interesting to read, and comparatively few in number. This point at once suggests that the local church needs a library of well-selected reference materials which may be made readily accessible to its workers.

f) The worker himself, and his need for inspiration and spiritual nurture, should not be forgotten. From time to time something should be included for his particular benefit, not to tell him what to do, but to inspire him to attempt it. If the worker can be aroused to the need and possibility of his own self-improvement, many of these other matters will take care of themselves.

V. Providing for the Several Agencies

One of the most troublesome problems for those making the curriculum of Christian education is that of providing properly for the several agencies through which any church carries on its program. They are all involved in the same task, but they work under widely varying conditions. These conditions include the amount of time available, the interval between sessions, the quality of leadership, the time of week, the time of year, the place of meeting, and the extent to which they are dominated by tradition.

The problem is one for the denominational and interdenominational curriculum committees who make the general plans, but it is even more a problem for the church. These agencies exist in varying numbers in any church, and an over-all curriculum plan for that church should make its allocation of responsibility in accordance with what is possible in its situation.

In the preceding chapter we suggested the specific contribution which each of these agencies might best be able to make. In so far as this affects the curriculum, it would seem that the following generalizations might be possible.

Since the Sunday school exists more generally in all churches, and almost always draws the largest constituency of any of the agencies, it should probably provide the basic curriculum. This will include the essentials of the Christian faith and life, running strongly to biblical, historical, doctrinal, and ethical content. These elements will not be absent from other curricula, but they will be supplementary to the Sunday school and will approach the same problems in different ways. In point of method, until present limitations of time and equipment are overcome, the Sunday school curriculum may have to make considerable room for a maximum of lecture, discussion, storytelling, and other types of "talking" methods, and a minimum of activity—not because this is the ideal, but because we must meet the practical situation as we find it.

The vacation church school may well capitalize on the religious values in nature because of its summertime setting. It may also turn in the direction of community needs and the cultivation of constructive citizenship, including relation to other churches. In point of method, the vacation church school is ideally suited for projects which require hours of time, following closely upon each other with a large measure of continuity, plenty of space indoors and out, and the freedom of the weekday to saw, hammer, sew, paint, dramatize, visit, and play.

The weekday church school, with its well-trained teachers and an atmosphere of work and study which closely approximates that of the public school, may well turn its attention in the direction of the mastery of the content of the Christian religion and its application to such problems as readily arise in connection with the public school experience. This is the more pertinent because the teaching of content is so inadequately done in most Sunday schools. It is here that attractive textbooks and supplementary materials should be used, in no wise suffering by comparison with public school materials. In point of method, the weekday school may go much further than most of the other agencies in the use of resource materials, discussions, projects, workbooks, and hard though interesting examinations.

The youth fellowship, because of its typically informal character and its dependence upon pupil leadership, may best give its major attention to the current life needs of youth in the field of personal problems, ethics, social issues, and religious perplexities. Let it depend on other agencies for more formal instruction in units of content. In point of method, there should be considerable variety, with now a talk, now a worship service rich in symbolism, now a discussion, a drama, or a project of service or social reconstruction. Furthermore, the curriculum should not ignore the increasing tendency in many churches to expand the youth fellowship program into many activities during the week, utilizing to the fullest the opportunities for Christian nurture found in wholesome recreational activities, special study groups, community work projects, projects of Christian service, intimate prayer fellowships, informal excursions to discover the facts about community life, definite action to attain social, economic, and political justice, and cooperation on an interdenominational basis with other Christian youth in the community to express the unity of the Christian fellowship.

This does not include all the agencies at work in the church but is sufficient to illustrate the problem of curriculum allocation.

VI. How May We Get Better Curricula?

The foregoing discussion leads to certain conclusions regarding desirable new developments in the curriculum of Christian education.

161

1. The curriculum must become more representative of the total life and interests of the church. It is the church which determines what is important in ritual, doctrine, history and literature, ethical ideals and Christian work. Christian education should reflect the "culture" of the church in these matters, just as any school reflects the culture of the society which it represents.

That is not to say that Christian education is to be merely a servant. It is a legitimate child of the church and therefore shares in its heritage and contributes to its progress. The function of any school worthy of the name is not just to reflect the status quo, but also to evaluate critically and to improve where improvement is needed and possible. Thus we may expect that an educational process which is within the interests and life of the church will not only impart what are regarded as the highest values, but also contribute to the emergence of new values.

The new conception of Christian education as the function of the church, and not of a half-dozen separate agencies, makes possible for the first time a comprehensive curriculum process which is true to the whole church. It follows that curriculum making will no longer be the sole prerogative of educational specialists. It will require the collaboration of theologians, biblical scholars, church historians, and specialists in other fields of the church's life and work. It will utilize the contributions of commissions on evangelism, social action, and the like, so that these interests may find their way in due measure into the curriculum. But the educational aspects of curriculum making will still be carried by those specifically trained for it. The Protestant churches of

America need to make more adequate provisions than have yet appeared for the training of editors and lesson writers. This is a part of the total problem of leadership for Christian education.

2. The local church must assume a larger share in curriculum making. This will not minimize the work of the national boards. It will enable these boards to bring their work to more effective fruition in the lives of the persons to be taught. Good materials for the guidance and use of local workers are essential. But an effective curriculum does not result until these materials bear fruit by becoming a true learning experience in a class or other group.

This suggests that a more intensive field program is needed, aimed at the curriculum problem in two ways: (1) to help churches grapple more effectively with their own curriculum needs, and (2) to interpret by personal contact and demonstration what is available by way of lesson materials and how they may best be used. Not the least important of the field representative's jobs is that of convincing churches that they must expect to make adequate expenditures for good materials.

With individual teachers, the program of leadership training needs to center more in curriculum. This will take the form of helping them to understand the fundamental principles of education on which the curriculum is based, showing them what this means for them and the groups they teach in terms of actual activities and procedures, and familiarizing them with the lesson materials themselves so that they may use them as was intended by the curriculum writers.

Most churches will do best to use one of the established curricula of their denominations. They need help in selecting the best for their purpose and to use it intelligently and well. But those churches who *can* do a more creative curriculum job should be encouraged to do so. Their procedure will be to develop an over-all course of study, built on the objectives they have selected, and in the light of the needs of their pupils, the abilities of their workers, and the possibilities within their church. Units of work will be described by departments and grades and for the several agencies working within each department. The best lesson materials available will be selected for use in the several units of the curriculum, and in areas where none are published, competent teachers may develop their own. Visual aids and other resources will readily find their proper place in this plan. The over-all plan will assure balance in units and movement toward the accepted goals.

3. A higher quality of curriculum materials than that which characterizes those commonly in use is urgently needed. Much improvement has been made in materials in recent years, but the procession still lags far behind that to which children and youth are accustomed in other fields and that which their Catholic and Jewish friends are having in their religious education.

The problem is partly one of dollars and cents. Churches will not buy the better materials, we are told. This difficulty arises from the expectation that church school materials must always circulate in huge quantities so that the price may be held at a ridiculously low figure. There are enough churches desiring a higher type curriculum to make a well-conceived venture of this sort a success. Evidence of this is to be found in the extent to which books like *The Story of the Bible,* by Walter Russell Bowie, and *The Church of Our Fathers,* by Roland Bainton, have been used in church schools, even though not primarily planned for that purpose. Moreover, it is not beyond the function of the agencies charged with providing the churches with good printed materials to make an initial subsidy for the welfare of the churches from which they draw their life.

This problem of providing better materials is one for Protestantism as a whole. It requires interdenominational cooperation in publication. A comparison of materials published by different denominations will show that there is little need for such separate publication, except in certain matters of doctrine, polity, and sacramental practice. The content and format reveal a surprising and monotonous similarity. To continue the practice of duplicating each other's efforts one step beyond the actual need for it is a disservice to the growing ecumenical spirit as well as to the best interests of the local churches.

What is here proposed is that instead of denominational varieties of curriculum materials we have a greater variety of materials from an educational standpoint. Thus it would be possible for local churches to select a series which is best suited to their tastes and abilities. The wider circulation which would result for any one series under cooperative publication and promotion would make possible the higher quality which is so much needed.

A new Protestant agency has recently been established by the denominational publishing houses from which much is expected. Known as the Cooperative Publishing Association, this agency is administered by the publishing houses, with the constant advice and counsel of editors, age-group workers, and other specialists from the denominations and the International Council. Its formation will greatly expedite the issuance of weekday, vacation, and leadership texts as well as other cooperatively produced material. Educational leaders have hailed this new and promising association with satisfaction and are giving it their hearty support, expecting that as it succeeds in its early ventures it will expand its facilities.

The new cooperative approach mentioned in the preceding paragraph should also make possible a more extensive and effective use of such newer resources as radio and visual aids. Visual education, in particular, is making a strong bid for inclusion as an integral part of the curriculum. Its proved effectiveness makes it imperative that the church incorporate its use in its work. Yet this movement (with the exception of printed pictures) stands almost wholly outside the regular curriculum services to the churches. No way has been found to make visual aids a part of the regular curriculum, with visual materials readily and inexpensively available. Each local church must make its own effort at inclusion of visual aids in its curriculum, frequently resulting in ineffective use and unfortunate effects on the curriculum as a whole. The problem involved here is too comprehensive and general for any one denomination to solve by itself. If traditional patterns and entrenched interests can be sufficiently transcended, we may move together into great new opportunities.

4. A serious effort to incorporate material for the home in a total curriculum plan needs still to be made. This will require much study and experimentation. It is really a part of the problem just discussed. The cost in time, effort, and money involved in making an adequate approach to this problem requires the united resources of Protestantism in cooperative endeavor.

Chapter V

The Family in Christian Education

*T*HE family is primary in God's economy. It is the most potent influence in the development of personality. It may be the most effective means of Christian education. Nowhere else may religion be taught so easily and with such abiding results as in the home.

The basic concepts of the Christian faith may come alive with meaning when they are interpreted in terms of family life at its best. God as Creator and Redeemer may well be understood in terms of the personal relationships of the home: the Father who understands and loves and with infinite patience guides his children. Our theological doctrines of freedom and grace may become meaningful realities when explained in the light of parental affection and responsibility. But if the home does not provide an ennobling and cooperative experience for children, how can they adequately understand the Christian idea of God as "Father"?

The ethical nature of the Christian gospel is often expressed in the analogy of family relationships. God is a Father of moral love; we are responsible children of God. Active good will and forgiving love characterize those who are Christians—"members of the family of Christ." Our social objectives are stated in terms of an all-inclusive family. But how can children and young people know what is meant by the extension of this spirit and purpose to community and world relationships unless they have a satisfying experience of Christian fellowship in the home?

Whether we wish it or not, learning constantly takes place within the family circle. It never ceases. Naturally, easily, and effectively the thinking and living of old and young are being shaped by the daily events of home life. Ideas are fashioned, and the emotional quality of the family relationship transforms ideas into prejudices, ideals, and purposes. The cumulative experiences of this intimate group determine lasting attitudes and habits.

The reality and quality of religion are constantly tested within the home. Concealment is difficult and often impossible. Life-changing influence is inevitable. Is the religion of adults a Sunday-morning-in-the-congregation event, or is it that which determines the daily decisions at home, at the office, in politics and industry? Is religion merely intellectual assent to words and phrases, or is it an active force in the full round of human experience? Is religion something which is merely professed, or is it lived?

Before the child can frame the question, he knows the answer. Throughout childhood and adolescence a boy's character may be more easily affected by association with his parents and brothers and sisters than by any other factor. He imitates the habits of the members of his family or reacts against the examples set him. In either case, he is learning from the life about him. He grows strong against the forces of evil, within and without, or he is denied that spiritual vigor necessary in a world of temptation and tension.

The home existed before the school. It antedated the Christian church. Among the Hebrew people it was a primary means of transmitting the culture of a people, a culture which was essentially religious. The school and the church in our modern civilization play a larger role than in earlier times, and their functions are not to be minimized. But they are supplementary or complementary. The home is still the first teacher in point of time. It is still the most influential teacher, but its teaching is too seldom definitely and effectively Christian. Whether we think in terms of recruiting strength for the church of tomorrow, of rearing a generation of young Christians, or of achieving a brotherly world, our hope and despair root in the home.

Some within the current movement of Christian education would hold that the home is the basic religious unit, as it is the primary social unit, and that the church is a fellowship of individuals and families. Others would insist that the church is the basic religious unit and that certain aspects of its life are cultivated and expressed in families. Still others might place the emphasis upon the individual's relationship to God, and would regard the church and the home as two areas in which this personal relationship is shared with others. But all would agree that the home and church are two of the primary social units through which God's will may be understood and realized. All would agree that education takes place in both and that this education should be definitely Christian. The primacy of the home and church is central in the Christian view of life. Any adequate program of Christian education, therefore, will be a comprehensive one, in which the home and church are two important agencies of Christian nurture.

II. The Home and the Church School

The home has virtually abdicated as a purposeful Christian teacher. Most if not all of the responsibility has been shifted to the church. The Sunday school was never intended to supersede the home as the teacher of religion. It began as a missionary or social agency with an educational purpose. At the outset it was for children who were denied the benefits of family or public school instruction. As its scope widened, its most loyal members came from church families. As time passed and it grew in influence, Christian parents left more and more of religious instruction to the Sunday church school.

Church people of our day do not rely upon their own spiritual resources as much as in other times; they have come to depend upon the printed aids supplied by denominational and other religious agencies. Quantities of such materials are available: prayer meeting suggestions, lessons for church school classes, guides for teachers in the church school, missionary and general religious literature. But there are few educational guides for the use of families in the home—families in which the needs of children are a paramount concern. And too few pastors and denominational officers seem to have recognized that the home is potentially the major teacher of religion.

It should be said that most parents probably try to teach their children their own conceptions of "right" and "wrong," and that large numbers of them earnestly endeavor to guide the young into "the good life." By wise and unwise methods, parents seek to shield their boys and girls from wrongdoing and attempt to inculcate a high degree of moral responsibility. They support character-building agencies in the community. One of the reasons that so many send their children to the church school is that these children may receive additional ethical guidance. But character education is one thing; Christian education is something more. It is at the point of *purposeful Christian* nurture that the modern home has been negligent.

Too much has been expected of the church school. Viewed from the limited perspective of biblical, historical, and theological information to be interpreted to the young, is it reasonable to expect the church school to do an adequate job in an hour or less of instruction a week? Considered from the standpoint of developing an intelligent and active faith, can it properly be expected that the Sunday program can succeed except as it buttresses the contagious religious influence of the child's parents? Surely, it is folly to think that even the best church school teaching alone will produce Christian character.

There are no sharper critics of the church school than the leaders of Christian education themselves. Some feel that the greatest hope for the future lies in improving the present church school so that it may become what it ought to be. Others are seeking a solution in experimental substitutes, such as the junior church, as the successor of the church school department. Still others believe that hope lies in an added hour each week, either as an expansion of the Sunday session or in cooperation with the weekday public school. But something more fundamental and radical is required.

Christian parents must become the chief teachers of religion. The locale of Christian nurture should be in the kitchen and parlor and bedroom and on the playground as well as in the classroom. The national leaders of the churches need to awaken to the fact that a major responsibility is to furnish help in the development of Christian family life. To perpetuate and expand the church school is a secondary objective. To grow genuine Christians is our first purpose. When the home undertakes the work of religious education seriously, fathers and mothers will become convinced that there is a supplementary place for the church school. Then, too, the church school will be able to lay hold of mature Christian teachers who possess the skill which grows from experience in teaching religion in the home.

III. The Impact of Secular Culture

The secular world impinges upon the church and home. The church has taken on too much the nature of the secular world. It needs to be pitted frankly against certain dominant forces of our social and industrial life. One of its functions is to be so uniquely and aggressively different that it will have a redemptive influence upon every aspect of society. When it is said that "the church" must do this, what is meant except that Christians, individually and collectively, shall reveal a different kind of life than is now characteristic of society? The problem of the religious education of the young roots in the lack of vital and intelligent adult religion. It may truly be said that a new era of family religion awaits the evangelization of adult Christians and of unchurched men and women.

Social life is always in process of change. These changes always influence the standards and practices of individuals, families, and the church. But in our day material changes have come so rapidly that our generation has felt the social impact more severely than in most periods of history. This is a transitional age, but to what is it a transition? Scientific progress accounts for much of the increase in the tempo of life, and it is agreed that this rapid change may not be true progress. Whether the modifications in ethical ideas are largely results of this scientific change or whether they are largely due to the insipidity of twentieth century religion may be a matter for debate. At any rate, the family and the church face an intensity of social pressure which greatly complicates their work of Christian nurture.

In grandmother's day family life was a close-knit unity. A home included children of various ages and often two or three generations of adults. They lived, worked, planned, rejoiced, and suffered together. Their home was their world. The economic problem was common to all members of the family, and all labored to solve it. Through this labor the children learned valuable attitudes and habits—attitudes and habits which were experienced in practice as well as explained by precept. The learning consisted of experience and interpretation. These attitudes and habits were part of the religion which was transmitted to the oncoming generation.

Clothes began with sheep. When the sheep were those on the family farm, hardly a child old enough to toddle was too young to help out in the first step of the process of getting trousers on his legs and a coat on his back. If a baby lamb was ignored by a lack-witted ewe mother, it was given to a six-year-old boy to feed and bring up. Not because psychologists had told parents—accurately and intelligently—that it is "good for children" to have the care of pet animals, but because the family needed the wool that the lamb when grown up would produce. . . .

As for the twelve-year-old boy sent out to give the flock their morning food and let them out from the barn into the right field, the responsibility put on him was not only actual but considerable. He was pulling his full weight in the family boat. Even more important than this, far more, was the fact that the work which he did was an apprenticeship to the work he would do in maturity. . . .

When the eighteen-year-old boy in an eighteenth-century American family put on a new pair of pants, he had earned them; not because it was good for his personality development, but because if he had not done his part of the work of producing them, there wouldn't have been any pants. In exactly the same way young people in the preindustrial period helped produce all that was needed, from soap to shoes, and hence learned how to produce. They acquired these necessary skills *without leaving home.* They were instructed by adults to whom they were personally known. And by the nature of the situation rather than by careful educational planning, the instruction given them was in graduated steps, adapted by long experience to the capacities of each age group.[1]

True, the close-knit family of past generations has been idealized. It produced frustrations as well as deep personal satisfactions. It taught much which was inadequate, restrictive, untrue. It failed to provide many of the physical, mental, and spiritual resources which people of all ages need in a rigorous and baffling world. Even if a return to the intimate fellowship, the self-sufficiency, and the cooperative activity of pioneer homes were possible, there is no certainty that people would live more spiritually in this materialistic age. And such a return is indeed impossible. But we must seek some substitute for those former relationships which produced

---

[1]Dorothy Canfield Fisher, *Our Young Folks,* pp. 20-22. Harcourt, Brace & Co., 1943. Used by permission.

undeniable values, and it is necessary to discover ways by which wholesome companionship within the family circle can be restored and maintained on a spiritual basis.

This needs to be attempted even though present-day conditions make it difficult for large sections of our population. The mobility of American families is, in part, accounted for by the facility with which people may travel great distances. It is an inevitable result, too, of our high-powered industrial organization, an aspect of economic insecurity. The war, of course, greatly accentuated the instability of family life. During the post-war period, uprooted families must again move. Tens of thousands of newly married men and women live in temporary homes, often under cruel circumstances. The best of people cannot escape the tragic effects of these social experiences. Even those with religious yearnings and lifelong habits of church attendance find it hard to maintain their self-respect, their faith, their loyalty to the church.

It is not easy today to try to picture or describe "the normal home." The extravagant mansion, the small single house, the crowded rooming house, the bandbox apartment, the trailer and emergency housing unit, the remote farmhouse, the sharecropper's shack—these and more are part of the picture. The church, then, faces the necessity of so adjusting its conception of its ministry that the rooted and the transient, the fortunate and the unfortunate, are served at the points of greatest need and by methods and resources appropriate to these needs. Its gospel must not be proclaimed in a vacuum or directed to a "once-was era." Nor must it despair of creating a redemptive type of life within homes which are not even houses. It has a social mission which includes the effort to secure wholesome living conditions for all people. It has an evangelistic mission of bringing God into the family fellowship wherever that family may live. It has an educational mission which embraces both of these and which also includes guidance in the teaching of religion at home.

The average family of today is a small two-generation group. Much of the day is spent away from home by all the members of the family, except the mother and very small children. The work of a small house or apartment requires less of the time of any person than formerly. There is little group activity in the home, and much of what remains is of the sweeping and cooking and errand variety. Little common effort is put forth to produce the goods which are necessary for subsistence. Money has a new place in our economy and an exaggerated place in our thinking. Everyone wants more money to get more of the things that are supposed to enrich life. Children grow up more aware of the worth of money as means to ends than of the worth of the ends themselves. Young people must have money in order to keep up with the crowd. If they go to work early in order to get this money, their sense of values is colored by their employers or by the employees with whom they associate— able teachers who are not conscious of what or how they teach. If they go to college, they may graduate with little sense of personal mission but with an avid desire to sit comfortably on top of the world.

The particular family belongs to one of the strata of a highly organized economic society. There is an all but universal desire to keep up with the Joneses or to climb above them. Beneath this ambition to rise ever higher in the economic world is the feeling of insecurity. This is reflected in table conversation, in the edginess of after-work hours, in the nervous tempo of daily experience, and in the accentuated class consciousness which divides the community.

Accompanying the radical change which has taken place in the world of work has come a comparable shift in ideas and ideals. The stern Puritan sense of duty has gradually given way to excessive freedom and a lawlessness of mind. Young and old get around and observe what others do and tend to join the uninhibited minority which has grown into a throng. The world of never-was is dramatically portrayed on the screen and over the radio and is "realistically" described both in "good literature" and in the lurid pulp magazines. This fictional world is accepted by many as the world which is and ought to be. Controlling loyalties which rooted in religion or social obligation or self-respect have weakened. Whether it concerns the observance of Sunday, the use of liquor, the relations between the sexes, the mutual responsibilities of members of a family, or attitudes toward one's fellow men, there often seems to be little or no difference between the Christian and the nonprofessing person. Even church families, more than they realize, take their view of life more from Broadway, Hollywood, Wall Street, and the omniscient commentators of press and radio than from the New Testament or the pulpit. The world is much with us—the bread-and-butter-and-cake world and the world of speed and thrills —much more with us than the world of the gospel and the Kingdom of God.

The discoveries of science present grave dangers for the oncoming generations, but they offer the home innumerable assets for the work of Christian nurture. The great classics of music are as free as the sentimentalities of current crooners. Thoughtful sermons by able preachers may be heard in the most remote home. Intelligent discussions on horizon-broadening issues are freely offered to the entire nation by the broadcasting chains. The automobile may be a means of taking families on educational journeys, on sheer pleasure trips which help to knit the group into the fellowship of love and understanding, and on missions of service. Money may purchase treasures as well as tawdry trinkets, permanent possessions which give continuous satisfaction as well as momentary pleasures which yield only ephemeral thrills. In an unbounded world community the mutual meaning of neighborliness may be so experienced and expressed as to have significance for all of the future. The "one family" era may indeed become the "one world" epoch if the home and church will use well their common opportunity. But its coming depends upon the readiness of the home to develop a new awareness of its mission, both for its own members and for a civilization which teeters between extinction and rich fulfillment of its destiny.

IV. Present Policy and Practice

The discussion thus far has put into words and into the present tense what is widely held with respect to the place of the family in Christian education. The denominational and interdenominational agencies of Christian education have accepted in theory the full implications of what has been said. Here, for example, are the words of the International Council of Religious Education, representing the Christian education forces of most of the Protestant churches of North America:

> As the primary and most intimate social group, the family is potentially the most important means of Christian education for all its members. . . .
>
> . . . .
>
> The nature and function of the family give it distinct advantages in Christian education. It has the growing person first, and it has him for the largest amount of time during the years of greatest responsiveness and modifiability. It brings to bear on him most effectively the education which comes from social participation and fellowship. It is in the most favorable position to make use of the learner's current interests and needs. It provides a constant living example of what it seeks to teach in Christian living.
>
> . . . .
>
> In view of the important place of the family in any comprehensive plan for Christian education, the establishing and sustaining of Christian families will itself become one of the goals toward which the efforts of Christian education will be directed. . . .
>
> The church and the family should stand in relationship as co-workers in Christian education, each doing that which it can best do. At its best, the church school may well represent the combined efforts of the people of the church to provide Christian education which is in continuous relation with what is being done in the families of the church.
>
> . . . .
>
> Thus church and family serve and support each other, not chiefly from duty or even from choice, but because they have so much in common in their functions and destinies. It is not a question of the church calling upon the family to help put over the church's program. Nor is it a question of the family calling in the church to make up for its failures or to take over a difficult part of its task. Rather it is a relationship of complete mutuality. The family finds its richest self-realization in the larger com-

munity of Christian families. . . . Together they seek to develop each person to his fullest spiritual capacities and to
extend that love and community to encompass all mankind
as children of one Father.[2]

From this expressed philosophy, it might be supposed
that Christian nurture centers as much in Protestant
homes as in Protestant churches, that the programs of
the denominations are made effective in these two loci
of Christian education. It would be natural to expect that
if this were true, the curriculum-making bodies would
take into account what should happen in both places;
that these bodies would produce outlines for materials
to be used in the home as in the church; that the training processes would reach parents as often as they serve
church school teachers; that denominational publishers
would provide as rich a variety of printed materials for
family use as for the church school; and that the field
forces of the churches would be skilled and concerned to
improve the work of religious education in the home as
in the church. Moreover, since the wider mission of the
church is so dependent upon the quality of family life it
would seem that all of the central leadership of the denominations would join the educational specialists in
seeking to lift the level of family life.

This is not the case. From the services rendered the
local church, one would suppose that these agencies
limit Christian education almost wholly to what is done
within the church. Curricula are planned for use within
the church, and suggestions and supplemental materials
for the home are largely in the nature of making the
church curriculum more effective, or carrying out its

[2]*Christian Education Today*, pp. 20-22. International Council of Religious Education, 1940. Used by permission.

implications in home activities. The ideal of closely graded groups is adhered to, with little recognition that some of the most profound religious and educational values are to be found in groups which include young and old, such as the family. Educational staffs are appointed with a view to leadership of work within the church. Although these leaders usually have a lively sense of the fact that persons learn in varied settings and circumstances, most of their efforts are directed toward improving the work within the church and through the enterprises which the church sponsors.

Not many denominations have full-time secretaries whose major work is in the area of the home. Such a department could hardly function apart from the age-group departments, but it could help constantly to focus the work of the entire staff upon the home as well as upon the church. If one were to compute the importance of education in the family, or education for family life, by the amount of money now spent by the boards in developing the home aspect of the religious program, the conclusion would be that the home is not of first importance in the thinking of religious educators.

Nor is much effort put forth to change the situation by training men and women for family life, or by preparing older young people for marriage. There is an extensive program for training the workers in the church, but no corresponding program of equivalent proportions to prepare parents for the important task of Christian nurture in the home.

The exception to this lack of material for the home seems to be the increasing amount of devotional material to be had. Interestingly enough, these ventures were rarely sponsored by the Christian education boards or in cooperation with them. Most of them are not graded for families with various ages of children. They are prepared on the adult level. Their interest is in family worship, through contemplation of a Bible passage, a sermonette, and common prayer. They seldom encourage activities and group experiences. Without underestimating the good which may come from the use of such devotional publications, it must be pointed out that a planned program of Christian education includes a variety of approaches and many additional types of experiences.

The reasons for this gulf between theory and practice are not hard to find. In the first place, it is always a slow process to install in practice what is clearly seen in theory. In the second place, the programs of Christian education were well established on an in-church basis before this new emphasis on the central place of the family became articulate. Transition is always difficult. There are growing indications, however, that the new emphasis is influencing the work of some boards of Christian education.

In local churches, the place of the family in Christian education is even less recognized than on a national scale. The trend has all been away from the home to activities within the church. Parents have thought they could thus discharge their religious obligations to their children. Churches have thought they could make up for lack of home nurture by more and better programs within the church, by their very nature dividing the family into different groups with no corresponding unitive influences.

There have been two unfortunate results from this tendency: First, the home has not been given the guidance it needs to come to its own self-realization as the basic institution of Christian education. There is plenty of complaint about what the home is not doing. There has been little constructive help through which parents might know what they ought to do and how to do it. This is a service the church ought to render. The home may become a center of religious influence, but it is not inherently so. Guidance is needed to help it realize and assume this, its highest function. Effort expended by the church at this point might bring manifold returns through extension of the influence of Christian nurture into numerous homes of the parish.

Second, because of ignorance or indifference to what is involved in Christian education, most parents have so resisted cooperation in what the church program is about that attendance, good conduct, lesson preparation, and other marks of a good school have become largely voluntary on the part of the pupils. Attendance of parents at meetings called to plan such cooperative effort is notoriously poor. Of course, the church school should be so inviting as to bring about voluntary participation as fully as possible. But it is to be doubted whether the effort involved in education can ever be made so attractive as to be consistently given by all pupils without a measure of home support. Without such effort on the part of pupils, it is vain to expect the results for which the church depends on its church school. Moreover, the nature of Christian education in its close relation to life and conduct and the limitations under which the church school works as to time are such as to require a joint effort of home and church if there is to be any measure of success commensurate with the need.

These considerations bring into sharp focus the problem arising when parents expect the church to give their children Christian education without their own participation in the church's program. While there are, of course, outstanding exceptions, there is evidence that, by and large, little of permanent value can be done for such children. Ralph N. McEntire of Topeka, Kansas, who has made a lifelong study of church school statistics, has presented the following evidence on this point:[3]

1. A study was made of the withdrawal from Sunday school of 700 persons under twenty years of age over a period of years, for other-than-good reasons. There were but three instances in which either the father or mother was enrolled in the school, or known to be actively supporting it.

2. Sixty-nine members of a church school were traced throughout their Sunday-school lifetime, from the beginners' department to the time of their withdrawal. The reasons for their withdrawal were listed. It was found that more than 80 per cent of the other-than-good reasons for their leaving stemmed directly from parental influence or example or act, intentionally or thoughtlessly or selfishly.

3. Studies of members of senior and young people's groups, tracing individual memberships through the local school or elsewhere when possible, show that more than 90 per cent of those who remain in the school, progressing through the various departments, come from homes where parents are church members and actively support the program.

[3]"Home Influence on Attendance," *International Journal of Religious Education*, April, 1943, p. 6. Used by permission.

4. Studies of church accessions of church school members indicate that some 90 per cent of these had a Christian home background on which the church could build. Many children from non-Christian homes go to Sunday school, but the schools seem unable to bring them to a commitment to church membership without home support.

The inevitable logic of these facts seems to be that if Christian nurture is to be given to children and young people, the major efforts must be directed to their parents.

V. RECOMMENDATION

It will be no easy task to revolutionize the thinking and practice of Protestantism so that the cultivation of family religion shall become a major concern of the entire church. The enlistment of millions of parents in an effort to provide sound Christian education for their children and to continue in a process of learning throughout all the years of adulthood is an undertaking which will take all the resources of national agencies, denominational and interdenominational, as well as those of the local churches. But it is doubtful whether any other effort will ultimately accomplish as much for young and old and for the Kingdom of God.

The Committee on the Study of Christian Education directed its one major recommendation in the field of family life to the International Council of Religious Education. It is stated in these words: "That the International Council of Religious Education examine its present and prospective program, its literature, and its structure to discover the degree to which home religion receives the attention which it deserves, and that it then revise its program, processes and structure so that the pre-eminence given to the family in its statements of basic philosophy is apparent in the full round of Council activities.'' This will lift the basic philosophy of the Council out of a booklet and put it at the heart of all its endeavors.

This is a necessary point at which to begin, for the Council is the agency through which the boards of Christian education of the denominations and the state councils cooperate. But it will be only a beginning. The Council itself does not publish lesson materials or make suggestions for the programs of local churches. From this point of beginning this study and action must carry into and through every national board, state and other local area organizations, and the local churches, until it actually reaches the ultimate point of effectiveness in the families of the continent.

This will mean that education for family life will assume an equal place with education for church and church school leadership, and that resources for Christian education within the family will be as much the concern of the agencies of Christian education as resources for church-centered religious education. It will mean that local churches in their planning will include the family in making provision for a total program.

There are many questions which require sustained thought and effort to answer. By what plan will the responsibility for Christian education be distributed to the church and the home respectively, with proper interrelation and correlation? What will be the nature of a curriculum for the home? Since there are such varied combinations of ages in homes, how can satisfactory plans be made for all of them? Will it be a formal series of courses to be used in the family in much the same way in which courses are used in the church? To what extent will the doctrinal and more factual elements of a curriculum be left to parental interpretation? How can consistency between the point of view of parents and church school leaders be achieved? Will the outlines, rather, propose a collection of suggestions for informal activities through which religious learning will take place—music, recreation, family festivals, projects of neighborliness? Will the problem of ill-prepared adult leadership become still more acute if a large part of Christian teaching is to center in the homes? Will much of the guidance be given by pastors as they visit in the homes, and will the national agencies be particularly concerned to develop resource materials for pastors?

As in all pioneer enterprises, the answers to such questions cannot be given with certainty without experimentation. Future committees will have learned much through the trial-and-error method in local efforts. Much of what will be done during the first years will be tentative. But the International Council has within its membership a body of leadership which is capable of projecting a home-and-church curriculum which will be at least as effective in its total field of operation as the church school curriculum now is within its sphere. Enough local churches are convinced of the need that there will be a ready response to any concrete leadership given them by their boards.

Subject to modification and improvement through further study and experience, the following suggestions for the content of the curriculum for the home may now be ventured:

1. A tying together of church and home efforts through interesting "homework" for children and youth, related

to what is being done in the church school, with a clear appeal to parents for their cooperation and practical clues as to how they may give it.

2. Considerable help on family worship, comprising actual materials and services, as well as guidance to parents in formulating plans for family devotions of their own devising.

3. Practical suggestions for realizing the spiritual values inherent in birthdays, homecomings, anniversaries, great days of the church year, national holidays, the planting of a garden, the lighting of a fire in the fireplace, etc.

4. Lists of materials for good home reading—some for parents, some for children, some for the whole family together.

5. Similar lists of pictures for the home, or the prints themselves, together with suitable interpretations and teaching suggestions.

6. Guidance in the use of music in the home to the ends of Christian education.

7. Occasional bulletins on radio programs, motion pictures, and special community events, calling attention to their significance for the religious life of the home. (These materials would doubtless have to be prepared locally.)

8. Resource materials and guidance for home fellowship, including games, crafts, hobbies, picnics, trips, and the like.

9. Help to parents in their age-old task of child rearing and home building, covering the accepted findings of child psychology and home economics and offering specific suggestions for the meeting of the most typical and recurrent situations.

To enable fathers and mothers to become skillful parents is a task of startling but thrilling magnitude. Who can tell but what seemingly indifferent parents may develop into good teachers if adequate printed resources, visual aids, radio programs, and other helps are made available as they try to do what they know they ought to do? In these helps, it is just as important to include material for the parents' own mental and spiritual growth as materials to help them in the guidance of their children. Mature men and women who have given little thought to their religious lives since youth need guidance to help them begin and continue in a process of Christian growth.

Books and booklets for personal study and for group discussion will be needed. An aggressive effort to maintain classes in parent education within the churches and on a community-wide basis will be supplemented by summer courses in training schools and institutes and by specialized conferences for parents. Pastors, parents, and other lay leaders will be helped to counsel young people contemplating marriage. City, county, state, provincial, and International Council conventions may again interest large numbers of laymen and laywomen because their programs will offer help to adults and young people of every home.

Protestantism has only begun to explore the possibilities of audio-visual education. There are great opportunities for home education through the directed use of excellent picture and story books which issue from the religious and secular presses. The radio has entrance to homes which the church never touches. Religious radio programs, prepared with all the dramatic and technical art which characterizes commercial programs, can capture a large company of the listening public. Inspiration to better living, broadening of social horizons, deep inner commitment—these are possible results of a single fifteen-minute dramatization on the air.

But the churches should be concerned with something more than gaining a fleeting listening audience; they should use the radio and similar media as instruments of Christian education. A good sermon may make a deep impression; a good book may leave the reader with a desire to make more of his life; a powerful dramatization may move the hearer to resolute purpose. One moment of prayerful purpose—and then what? Christian education is a process; it is more than a series of incidents and moments.

VI. Conclusion

The burden of this chapter is that Protestant religious education in America is too closely confined within the pattern of the church school. Too much of it is expected to take place within the church building. More is demanded of the church school and of the church-centered activities than can be thus accomplished. Not enough is expected of the home.

The church school may have a rebirth of power if the church will go to the people where they live, if it will help them to establish and maintain a normal religious life within the home. Once parents become aware that the church is interested in helping them to share family life at its highest level, once they experience the satisfactions which intelligent Christian family life can afford, many may be convinced that what goes on in the church on Sunday is of supreme importance.

Despite the recent emphasis on the need of reaching

the unreached half of America, little progress has been made in the solution of this acute problem. Not much effort has been made to go where people are. The church cannot rest content as long as so many people remain absent from the house of worship. It is possible, however, that more people would be interested in the church if the church seemed more interested in the homes. It is a fact that many families cannot attend church regularly or send their children to church school regularly, because of distance or because of conflict with other family obligations. Modest experiments are now in progress which seek to establish "church schools in the home" or neighborhood church schools. Marked success attends some of these efforts. They are indicative of what may be done upon a much wider scale.

Protestantism is committed to the point of view that parents should rear their children as Christians. It does not accept the idea that it is the sole responsibility of specially ordained or elected priests or teachers to understand and interpret the will of God. Both the privileges and responsibilities of the universal priesthood of believers belong to the laymen and laywomen of our churches. Understanding and skill are required of those who are to teach the Christian religion, but it is the business of all Christians to learn how to grow and how to help each other to grow in the Christian life. Particularly is this an inescapable task of parenthood.

Through this effort concentrated in the homes, Christian education may enlist the support of a large part of the laity of the churches because it will concern itself with what is clearly the business of everyone, instead of seeming to be a matter for the faithful few who maintain the traditional Sunday school.

Chapter VI

Leadership for Christian Education

*T*O DEVELOP and conduct a program of Christian education requires workers who have the necessary personal qualities and who are consecrated and trained. The success of all that has been proposed, in any particular church, depends on the solution of the problem of leadership in that church.

We have defined Christian education as being fundamentally the Christian community sharing its life with its members, young and older—its traditions, its experiences, its hopes, its faith, its mission. This means that every person in the Christian fellowship is at one and the same time a learner and a leader. Each comes to his own understanding and appreciation of the Christian faith and life and, in turn, shares it with others. As people become more mature they are able to contribute proportionately more as leaders, but this should never blind us to the fact that everyone in the fellowship continues also to be a learner.

In this sense the education of workers for Christian education includes everyone in the church. Each should progressively understand the basic nature and function of the fellowship in which he is set so that he may participate the better in the achievement of its spirit and purpose. Theoretically at least, each should also take some responsibility for the work which must be done by the church if its mission is to be fulfilled. Some will be teachers, some will be administrators, some will be collectors and keepers of money, while some will merely be doorkeepers in the house of the Lord. The preparation of workers for the church should apply broadly to all who take leadership responsibility, and not simply to those who are working in the program of Christian education.

We have defined the Christian fellowship of the church as extending to the families of the church and including them. We have maintained the position that the major work of Christian education will be done in the family. Thus, the preparation of men and women for effective Christian nurture in the home is also a part of the total problem of the training of workers for Christian education.

More specifically, however, the program of leadership education is usually directed to those who are responsible for Christian education in the local church and to those aspects of it which involve numbers of churches in their denominational or interdenominational relationships. There is need here for both professional and lay workers. While the lay worker came first, and most of the effort at leadership education has been directed to him, our discussion will deal first with the professional worker because of his necessary relation to the solution of the lay worker problem.

I. Professional Workers

It is difficult to draw a line between the professional worker and the lay worker because they do not constitute two distinct categories. In general, we mean by professional workers those who have had more extensive training and experience than can be expected of lay workers, and generally the amount of time which they devote to the work is such that they are on an employed basis, either full-time or part-time. There will be exceptions to this classification, for there are some lay workers who are better prepared for their work than many professional workers, and some who give more time voluntarily than some professional workers who receive a salary. Also there are some who classify as lay workers who are paid a small stipend for their services.

There has been much discussion as to the relative merits of having professional or lay leadership for Christian education. On the one hand are those who feel that the work involved is of such a technical nature that only those who are professionally trained and adequately compensated can be expected to carry it on satisfactorily. On the other hand are those who feel that the traditional procedure of having Christian education in the hands of lay people has such advantages that it should be rigorously adhered to. The position which we are assuming is that both types of workers are needed. It is not likely that a local church will develop the kind of program described in the preceding pages unless there is a measure of professional leadership. On the other hand, there will be rare instances in which a sufficient number of trained workers are available to put the entire work on a professional basis, or adequate funds to pay such professional workers for their services. Moreover, we recognize also that there are values in the use of lay workers in Christian education, in the very fact that they are *lay*.

1. *The minister.*—It will be rather generally accepted that the minister is the key person in the local church. He is now, and in any foreseeable future will continue to be, the only professionally trained person in the vast majority of our churches. Even in those churches which

can employ additional members of a staff, the nature of Christian education is such that the minister must still be vitally related to it.

The minister has been slow to accept this position of leadership in Christian education. In some cases the people of the church have been slow to accord to him the opportunity for such leadership. Both of these are the result of a misunderstanding of the nature of Christian education and the place which it holds in the total work of the church. It follows from this attitude that ministers are often inadequately trained for the work in Christian education. Perhaps the majority of them would admit that the task of the minister is so complex that they find themselves inadequately trained at many points. But this inadequacy is most serious where it prevents their fulfilling the educational function because Christian education is so basic to the whole work of the church. That ministers can and will assume educational leadership in their churches when properly trained for it is attested by the thousands of them who are in the forefront of leadership in all denominations.

The theological seminaries must bear a large part of the responsibility if ministers continue to be inadequately trained in Christian education. Being one of the most recent arrivals, Christian education is generally accorded a minor place in the seminary curriculum and an equally minor place in the appreciation of other faculty members and students generally. Even where it has been granted adequate recognition, the fact still remains that a few elective courses in Christian education added to the rest of the seminary curriculum will not solve the problem.

If the position which has been taken in this book on the central place of Christian education in the function of the church is sound, and if the primary function of the seminary is the training of effective ministers, then Christian education, together with preaching and public worship, pastoral work, and church administration, should presumably be the organizing center for the seminary curriculum. This would in no sense minimize the importance of the other courses in the curriculum. It would, however, serve as a new orientation for the student's seminary studies, for it would enable him to view all the work which he is doing in terms of the task for which he is preparing. It is granted, of course, that much of the work of the seminary is for the man himself, to make him a better informed and a more deeply religious person; but these studies must finally come to fruition in what the minister does in bringing the people of his churches, old and young, into the Kingdom. Seminary study should be at the highest level intellectually at which the student is capable of working, but at the same time it should not lose sight of the fact that it must fit him to become an interpreter of religion to the common people.

One of the most important aspects of the minister's training should be in the underlying principles and practice of the development of lay leadership. If he should not hold himself aloof from the church's educational program, it is just as true that he should not himself attempt to do all that needs to be done. His success in any permanent sense will be measured by his ability to discover, inspire, and train lay workers. Perhaps the word "discover" has been used inadvisedly, for in many cases these workers do not exist except potentially. In a very real sense the pastor must become a creator of leadership vision and ability. In this he is not far from the insight of his Master, who saw potential abilities in very ordinary men and spent a great deal of his effort in inspiring and training them to carry on his work after him.

2. *The minister of Christian education.*—In the past half century a new profession in the church has been emerging, that of a ministry in Christian education. During the first part of this period there was rapid development in this direction. Numerous young people were presenting themselves for this type of Christian service, and churches were experimenting with this new approach to the leadership of their work. Utopian dreams were held concerning the results which might be expected from this new ministry.

These dreams were, of course, doomed to disappointment. The reasons for this are many. It is the habit of new movements to claim too much for themselves. A new movement is also bound to make mistakes in its first period of experimentation, and Christian education has made its share of them. Christian educators were sometimes arrogant—they had been told that theirs would be the most important work in the church, and they believed it and acted accordingly. They were sometimes inadequately trained, particularly at the point of the history and tradition of the church and the content of Christian belief. On the other hand, churches also made mistakes. Some made too great a separation between the work of the minister of Christian education and that of the pastor. In some cases the minister of Christian education was expected to do almost anything, including secretarial work and janitorial service. Always the pastor was given the position of highest honor and prominence, and when the Christian educator's own sheer ability chanced to draw some of the limelight to him, jealousies developed which made working together impossible. This could have been very different if the pastor had accepted his minister of education as a co-worker to whom he might extend the benefit of his own wider experience and with whom he might share the hopes and dreams of his church.

At about the time when a restudy of the place for the minister of Christian education in the church might have been possible, a financial depression hit the country, with the result that churches with decreasing incomes often followed the expedient of dropping their employed worker in Christian education. This was the easier to do because of the growing doubt concerning his usefulness which has just been considered. Thus the whole movement of Christian education fell into a measure of disrepute, and a promising new profession was blasted.

More mature consideration has made it clear that whatever may be thought of the early efforts in a professional ministry of Christian education, there is a work to be done in every church which requires the kind of service for which these men and women were called. In the smaller church this service must, of course, be rendered by the minister. In a larger church an associate to the minister will be needed, who, in close cooperation with the minister, will carry the major responsibility for the educational program. In increasing numbers, churches are realizing this. In the meantime, however, the recruiting of workers in Christian education has broken down with the consequence that the churches desiring ministers of Christian education are having great difficulty in finding them. The number of churches desiring the services of ministers of Christian education is much greater than the supply, and the consequence is that there has been strong competition for those that are available.

It would seem that the opportunity to serve the church in Christian education would make a great appeal for life commitment to both young men and young women. The church has, however, shown far less initiative and foresight in recruiting and training for this type of service than in selecting and training missionaries. Whereas the missionary has status and security, the professionally trained worker in Christian education has neither. He has only confused standards, inadequate recognition, poor salary, almost no job security, little help in placement if it becomes necessary for him to make a change; and there is a tendency to regard him as superannuated by the time he reaches middle life. These conditions make it difficult to encourage young people to enter this profession. The church must face this liability and change these conditions if it is ever to have an adequate supply of professionally trained workers in Christian education.

The training of the minister of Christian education should be equivalent to that of the minister, with the exception that he would take more specialized work in education, whereas the minister's specialization is in homiletics, public worship, and the care of a parish. This standard presumes three years of graduate work and requires professional and financial recognition accordingly.

The question may well be raised whether there is a place for professional workers in Christian education with less highly specialized training than that indicated in the preceding paragraph. It is pointed out that teachers in public education may take a course in a teachers' college leading to the bachelor's degree and thereby be prepared to enter upon professional service. The answer would seem to depend on the amount of guidance and supervision which such workers may expect to receive. In a church in which the minister is competent and willing to give extensive guidance and help to the minister of Christian education, it is quite possible that a college graduate with a minor in Christian education could well carry on such work. The same is true of teachers in weekday church schools under competent supervision. The time has passed, however, when a few courses in educational method may be expected to prepare a person to become a professional leader in Christian education. The Christian educator must first of all be competent in the whole field of the Christian religion before he can become an adequate teacher of that religion. Equally impossible is it for the person whose training does not include specialized courses in Christian education to lead his church in this field. The three-year seminary course which has become standard for ministers, with a major in Christian education, is a minimum for the preparation of professional leaders in Christian education.

The work of the minister of Christian education will vary widely in different churches. There are, however, certain constants which should mark his work. He is the executive officer of the board of Christian education, on the one hand guiding its study and work, and on the other hand carrying out its decisions. He takes chief responsibility for the over-all curriculum, for it is his business to see the program of the church as a whole for which curriculum must be planned. He is the director of leadership education, inspiring and guiding the lay workers and helping them to find the necessary resources for their work. He maintains a close contact with the home, developing the desirable home-church cooperation and helping the home wherever possible in the discharge of its work in Christian nurture. He is usually the counselor of the youth of the church, but here great care should be taken that young people do not lose contact with the senior minister of the church.

3. *Other professional workers.*—Much of what has been said about recruiting, training, professional standing, salary, and security applies also to other professional workers in Christian education. A few of the fields for which such professional workers are now being used, and in which more are needed, are the following:

a) Beyond the ministry of the local church, there is need for a great number of highly trained and experienced professional workers to serve the denominational boards of Christian education and the councils of churches and Christian education. This calls for workers who by native talent, training, and experience are competent as executives, age-group specialists, field workers, editors, and leaders in special fields such as audio-visual education, dramatics, Christian social service, and many others. A fruitful local church experience is an important prerequisite to such wider leadership.

b) There is a pressing demand for trained leadership in weekday religious education, now expanding much more rapidly than the supply of competent leadership. We may predict that if the Protestant church is not willing to furnish an adequately trained and adequately paid teaching force for weekday schools of religion, it will lose this great opportunity through neglect and inefficiency. We venture to suggest that if we could give more assurance at the point of salary and security we might recruit an increasing number of trained and experienced public school teachers for work in the weekday school. With a minimum of training and with skillful supervision, these teachers would prove to be most effective.

c) The vast expansion of vacation religious education is a great challenge to the development of leadership. The interest which many vacation church schools have been able to draw from the children, and the effectiveness with which they have carried on their work, has in large degree been due to the high quality of their leadership. Here again the church is faced with disappointment in a great opportunity if it is not able to continue to furnish good educational leadership.

A phase of vacation religious education is the work carried on by summer camps and conferences of all sorts. Even during the war years the number of junior and intermediate camps increased by leaps and bounds. It is conceivable that in the very near future, camps and conferences for juniors, intermediates, and young people, and for adults as well, will be within the reach of every local church. Here a high degree of skilled leadership is needed. These camps and conferences are one of the most effective media for Christian education. But Christian education will not result if these camps and conferences are made merely an outing experience, valuable as that might be.

d) In the field of youth work in the local church it is becoming apparent that much more emphasis should have been placed upon the training of adult counselors of youth. In all the years that we have concentrated upon young people themselves we have neglected to enlist and train a sufficient number of adult counselors. Consequently, many a youth program in a local church has failed for lack of adult participation.

e) Leadership education classes and schools are also greatly in need of trained teachers. This is the more true because of the recent efforts to make such courses truly laboratory or workshop experiences. The present demand for demonstration teachers far exceeds the number available, and it is likely that this demand will increase.

f) Another type of worker for whom there is a great need is the specialist in a given field who is available for field service. The minister who takes educational responsibility for his church will soon find that he faces problems on which his church needs more expert guidance than he is able to give. It should be a simple matter for him to call in the proper specialist from somewhere in his community who, under his guidance, would help with such problems. This is a part of the problem of field organization which will be discussed in Chapter VIII, but the need should be recognized as a part of the total problem of providing Christian education with adequate professional leadership.

4. *Part-time workers.*—Many of the needs which have been discussed can be met by part-time workers, provided they are adequately trained. In their case the word "professional" should apply primarily to the type of training which they have had rather than to their being on a salaried basis. In fact, for some of the types of work which have been described, there is a distinct ad-

vantage if the person engaged in it is also having a wholesome and creative experience of his own in actual church school work, or as a parent.

It is possible that in many communities there are persons who could be secured by churches to give them part-time service of a highly professional character, when they are unable to engage a full-time minister of Christian education. No doubt there are people who would undergo the necessary training to qualify themselves for such service, if the opportunity for the service were offered them. This suggests a field for long-term planning which might well be more fully explored.

II. LAY WORKERS

The Protestant church has chosen to carry on its major work in Christian teaching by the use of its own people. No matter what may be one's opinion of the wisdom of this policy, it does confront us as a fact with which we must work. It is not likely that a drastic reversal of this policy will take place in the near future.

There are at least three distinct advantages which may be set down to the credit of this policy: (1) it is in the spirit of the Christian fellowship that its members should assume the responsibility for the various expressions of that fellowship, including its interpretation to the young; (2) assignment to work in Christian service is one of the means through which growth in Christian living may be made, and the highest type of such assignment is that of teaching the faith to others; (3) other things being equal, a positive factor is added to teaching when it is done on a voluntary basis and when the pupils know that what is taught comes from the overflow of the teacher's life and work as they see it in his everyday activity.

But it does not follow that *any* lay person may become a teacher of religion. Assuming a basic devotion to Christ and the church, there are still certain personality factors which are necessary for leadership. Moreover, teaching is an art which requires a high degree of skill, not only in "rightly dividing the word of truth," but also in developing an experience within individuals and groups. Consequently it will always be necessary to call certain people out from among the total church constituency to be the leaders in Christian education.

1. *Motivation.*—The Protestant principle of the use of lay persons to teach religion operates on the optimistic assumption that in any church there are men and women in sufficient numbers and with adequate ability to do this. We believe that this assumption is justified. But how are we to get those who are chosen for the purpose to accept such responsibility? How are we to get them to undergo the necessary training to make themselves competent? This involves the question of motivation.

Let us first recall our conception of the basic foundation for Christian education in the Christian fellowship. Once this basis is understood and accepted by the people of the church, we have the necessary grounds for calling into the work of teaching those who are best qualified. Whatever caused them to join this Christian fellowship, and leads them now to be loyal to it and active in it, should be the adequate motivation for them to render to the fellowship that service for which they are best qualified.

That the appeal of voluntary service strikes a responsive chord in the hearts of many people is evidenced by the large amount of voluntary work which is done in any community in times of great emergency such as war and in other cases of community need. There is a tremendous appeal in the urgency of work which needs to be done for the safety or welfare of the community. Not only are many hours given to the work of the Red Cross, air raid warden service, community chest, service organizations, clubs, and other interests, but also those called into such service will spend hours of time in preparation for doing their work effectively. Yet no appeal for voluntary service should be more insistent and more attractive to lay people than that of their own churches. It is unfortunately true that very often the ablest persons have their activities drawn off into community agencies, while the less able need to find their satisfaction in service within the church. (This may be one reason why there is so much maneuvering for prestige in many churches.) This should not be. Anyone whose life is committed to the Lord Jesus Christ should place service in his name first, and there is no greater service in his name than that of teaching his spirit and word.

There are, no doubt, many reasons which motivate people to render voluntary service—some high, some low. It seems, however, that the only adequate motivation for service in Christian education is that of the need and the opportunity, which should make an adequate appeal to every loyal church member. This major motivation may be supplemented by such things as a wholesome fellowship of the workers in Christian education, recognition on the part of the church, provision for attractive working conditions, a dignified and personal invitation from the church, indicating the ground on which this particular individual has been chosen.

2. *Challenge.*—A second step in the making of effective workers is to challenge them to a high type of service. There is an initial danger that lay people called into the teaching work of the church will tend to duplicate the methods which were used with them when they were children. This danger can be avoided if these new workers are given an insight immediately into the Christian education program as it now is and what it is seeking to accomplish. This will be done through personal conference at the time of appointment and continued through arranging for them to attend conventions, conferences, institutes, and training classes, encouraging them to read books and magazines, showing them how their lesson materials make provision for a new type of class procedure.

Sometimes this will mean that something must happen to the whole structure of the educational program of the local church. How can we expect lay workers to be greatly concerned with adequate preparation for and high devotion to their task if nothing really important ever happens? To the creative person placed in such a situation all that we say about his need for training is but empty words. No wonder that he will soon be drawn off to the more exciting activities of his lodge, service club, or other community agency.

One of the most effective challenges to creative work comes through participation in program planning. Herein lies the greatest service of the workers' conference and the group conferences by church school departments. Through such participation in the study of needs, planning of program, evaluation of work, the workers will receive a new insight into what it is all about. Once given a challenging purpose for the things which they are to do, they can be trusted to find the necessary ways and means of getting it done.

3. *Training.*—Training for leadership in Christian education involves two aspects. One is that of the mastery of the content of the field in which the teaching is to be done, and the other is the effective use of the techniques of leadership through which the desired results may be achieved. These are again divided into two phases each, namely: *(a)* the general content of the Christian religion and the specific content of the particular course which is to be taught; *(b)* the general basis of method and the specific procedure to be used with pupils of a particular age in a given situation with a specified type of curriculum.

This suggests a problem of training so vast that one wonders whether it can ever be done on a voluntary basis. We must admit at once that it can never be done adequately. To begin with, we must assume that through the fifteen or more years that a particular worker has been associated with his church, he has already achieved a fair degree of mastery of the Bible and other phases of the religious heritage. Unfortunately this is often a very precarious assumption, but it must nevertheless be made.

Specific training must then still be given in the particular content in which a worker is to work and in the methods by which his work is to be done. This training will be provided in two ways. First, there will be training courses, held either in his own church, a community training school, or a summer school. Through these courses, with their use of the prevailing educational techniques of textbooks, recitations, examinations, etc., he may make a systematic study of the subject. Second, there will be in-service training in the form of guidance at the various points of need. This will start with an interpretation of the lesson materials which he is to use. Throughout the period of his service, there should be frequent personal conferences to help him in making the best possible use of the general knowledge which he has acquired and in best meeting the specific problems of the particular situation in which he is placed.

This second type of training is important if courses in leadership education are to bear fruit in teaching practice. In the nature of the case, courses must be more or less general, adapted to the needs of different workers from different situations and different schools. What do these courses mean in application to a particular worker? It is here that practical guidance is needed. Another way of bridging this gap between study and practice is the laboratory school, which is increasingly used as a means of leadership education.

Perhaps the most effective training for service is self-training. The mere pursuit of courses of study and the participation in conferences will not make any worker the expert which he should be. It is only when he goes beyond the requirement of courses and becomes so immersed in his own work that he will proceed on his own initiative to study and experiment that he will become truly a creative teacher. When this stage is reached, the hours voluntarily and joyously devoted to the work of the church will go far beyond anything which justice could possibly require. It is because of the numbers of workers who have reached this stage of interest that we express our hope for the future of the church school under voluntary leadership.

4. *Supervision.*—The term "supervision" is applied to those activities which are intended to improve the work of the church school. They concern themselves with the development of better working conditions and better curricula, but they are primarily directed to the guidance of workers into more effective service. Supervision is probably the most hopeful approach to the training of lay workers.

Supervision is primarily the work of the minister of Christian education in churches which have such. In others the responsibility for supervision must fall to the pastor, the general superintendent, the department workers, and others who may be specifically appointed for this purpose. Sometimes it is possible to find among the lay members of the church a man or woman who has had the necessary training and experience to serve as a supervisor and who would prefer to give his or her time to that kind of activity rather than holding an office or teaching a class. One competent person appointed to this phase of leadership development may greatly improve the work of a dozen teachers and be one of the most fruitful avenues of approach to new workers.

One of the most persistent problems in the training of workers has been that of making these workers conscious of the need for training. Large numbers of them never enter training classes. Others who do are unaffected by the experience because they say that there was nothing in those courses which touched their need.

If we may assume that a worker is genuinely interested in his job, we may then assume also that he will be interested in learning how to do it with greater satisfaction. In other words, the key to motivating that worker to take training lies in helping him to do his work better. It is through supervision that these needs of workers can best be discovered and the necessary help given to meet them. It may be that the worker himself is not even conscious of receiving training. He is having the thrill of a new experience in studying his pupils, setting the aims for his work, and planning materials and procedure to realize his aims. Through it all he is becoming a more competent worker, and it makes no difference whether we call it by the name of leadership training or not.

A by-product of this type of training will be that the whole program will be related more effectively to the local church. There has been a considerable swing in public education toward an emphasis upon adapting the educative process to the particular factors in the situation in which education is going forward. This approach may be even more effectively applied in the church school, because conditions vary much more widely from church to church than they do from school to school.

III. Principles of Education for Workers

The principles of teaching which apply to the education of pupils also apply to the education of workers. If the need of the pupil is the law of the school, then the need of the teacher is the law of the teacher training school. If the life situations of the pupil are important in teaching, then the life situations of the teacher —his pupils, his class, his classroom, his lesson course— are important in the training of the teacher. There are, however, three specific principles of procedure which apply in particular to the training of workers.

1. *The Christian foundation of leadership development.*—The training of workers for Christian education seeks to help those workers nurture growing persons in the Christian life. It must therefore be founded on Christian assumptions. With all due recognition of what we may learn from the process of general education, we must still ask whether the practice of Christian education should have its own distinctive purpose, procedure, and content. We have maintained that the Christian religion has things to say about God and man, the nature and purpose of existence, which are central to the Christian faith and therefore must be central in Christian teaching. Therefore Christian leadership education must be distinctive in purpose, content, and method so as to prepare teachers of the *Christian* religion. In method it has certain values to preserve, certain spiritual ends to maintain, which are based upon its theory of man and the meaning of life.

The training of teachers therefore involves more than acquaintance with effective methods and mastery of the body of content material. Christian teaching requires a background of experience in the Christian faith. Teachers need growing appreciation of what is involved in a Christian approach to life. This does not mean simply a lay interpretation of systematic theology. It involves a grounding in religious experience which gives specific character to the whole enterprise for Christian teaching at all levels.

Teachers need to learn how to approach their students from the standpoint of their needs; but they also need instruction which will clarify their own belief and give definiteness to the Christian faith which inspires every teaching project within the church. Only then will they be able to increase their pupils in the knowledge of the will of God and the mind of Christ and deepen their experiences so as to spiritualize their attitudes, appreciations, hopes, and purposes and strengthen their faith.

2. *Content and method.*—There has been needless debate about the relationship between content and method in Christian teaching. No one teaches without content or without method. Unless we have effective content, we have no purpose for teaching; unless we have effective method, we have no way of making the content creative and meaningful for the pupil.

Content is not simply knowledge about religion. Content for Christian education is the good news of salvation. It is a "knowledge" of the word of God, not only in the mind but in the heart, and it is an understanding of the major purpose of the church in the redemptive process. To be "Bible centered" is not sufficient. It is not the use of the Bible in teaching, but how it is used, why it is used, and to what issue in daily living that makes the difference.

Method must serve a redemptive purpose. Given the view of content which we have tried to suggest in the two preceding paragraphs, the aims can be attained only through appropriate method. Content and method become integral parts of a total process. There has been far too much use of methods which have not been in keeping with the spiritual purpose of Christian education. That is why it is partly true at least that the church school has sometimes served only to inoculate children and youth against a vital religious experience and to give them and their parents the illusion that they have had Christian education, when in fact they have had only a smattering of information about religion.

3. *Learning through experience.*—Endless discussion has been given in leadership education courses to the "experience centered" principle in education. All too often these leadership training courses themselves have not proceeded by this principle. As a consequence there has been much loss of effectiveness and failure of carry-over from such courses into the practice of the teachers in training.

We have already suggested that in-service training through supervision is one of the most effective means of combining training and practice in the local church. It remains true, however, that in many local churches there is no one to give adequate supervision. Moreover, many local churches do not present an adequate situation in which the workers may receive the kind of training which they ought to have. This suggests that provision be made for training through observation and practice under conditions which are educationally beyond the possibility of the local church to supply.

The laboratory school is the best approach to this type of training. Such schools are usually held in relation to summer schools of religious education. Students enrolled for the laboratory school spend a part of the day in the study of the pupils, the methods, the materials, and the administration of the department in which they are specializing and a part of the day in observing the actual teaching of children by competent demonstration teachers. Preceding the demonstration teaching, they have an opportunity to share with the teacher the plans for the session, and following it they have an opportunity for discussion of the session which they observed. In some cases the more advanced students may participate in the teaching at certain points of the session, though this opportunity is not necessarily available to all the students.

Something approaching the laboratory school needs to be made readily available in every community. It does not seem impossible to suppose that a council of churches might select certain churches which would be willing to become demonstration centers and give them the necessary help to make their program worthy of observation. The churches of the community would then make arrangements for their teachers to utilize these centers for observation, and teachers of training classes would similarly utilize this experience for observation. In some local churches, one or more classes might be designated as observation centers for the teachers of that church, provided this could be done without incurring jealousy of other teachers toward those who are the demonstration teachers.

IV. Opportunities for Training for Service

Over a century ago it was concern for better teaching that led to the development of lesson materials in which helps for the teachers were provided. Source materials were developed in the form of well-known systems of teachers' aids, some of them still in use. The first national Sunday school conventions, held in 1832 and 1833, were partly for promotion, partly for the inspiration and training of teachers. The popular county and state Sunday school conventions, famous for a century, sought to lift the level of teaching, particularly among laymen.

In 1903 the first secretary of teacher training was appointed and the first elementary standards approved. With the advent of graded lessons, the Graded Unions began to be organized throughout the country, chiefly in cities, and helped greatly to improve the work with children through the adaptation of materials to the needs and interests of children. But most of the early emphasis was on what to teach rather than on how to teach. Teaching was almost wholly content centered. It is only within the last quarter century that attention has shifted to method.

The First Standard Course in Teacher Training called for fifty lessons with at least twenty lessons on the Bible. A three-year training course was outlined in 1916-17 and adopted by the International Sunday School Association. This course assumed that teachers had elsewhere acquired the basic knowledge of the Bible and other fields of Christian knowledge and devoted itself to guidance in the teaching of these materials. It provided for units on "The Pupil," "The Teacher," "The School," "The Life of Christ," "The Teaching Values of the Old Testament," "The Teaching Values of the New Testament," "Training the Devotional Life," and others.

The standard leadership training curriculum which, with some modification, is used today, was adopted in 1923. It consists of first, second, and third series courses, leading at various stages to marks of attainment in the form of certificates of progress. Third series courses are not extensively used, but first and second series courses are widely in use. In order to provide for a wide variety of needs, the custom has been followed of listing a considerable number of courses, appropriately grouped, rather than simply specifying certain required courses. Thus there are now fifty-two first series courses and 110 second series courses, all listed in the current Bulletins on Leadership Education of the International Council.[1]

To receive credit for the taking of these leadership courses, a student must meet certain standards of work, and the courses themselves must be offered under standard conditions. To receive a certificate of progress for the completion of the work in any particular series, the student must complete a certain combination of courses from various groups so as to provide for balanced training specialization in his own division of work. Significantly, the taking of courses is only one phase of leadership education, for the certificates of progress are awarded only after other conditions of participation in the work of the church, Christian growth, and service in the church school have been met. Care is taken to emphasize the fact that training must go on continuously, rather than providing simply for the taking of a number of courses in a limited time, on the basis of which the teacher may consider himself adequately trained.

In accordance with the genius and practice of the International Council, these leadership education curricula are cooperatively planned and standardized. The courses are in the standard curriculum through official action of the denominations which cooperate in the Council. These denominations are free to use them as they wish. Most of the cooperating denominations use these standard curricula almost in their entirety, though in some cases there are slight modifications, and in some cases

---

[1] See Bulletins Nos. 501 and 502, describing the first and second series courses respectively.

the addition of specifically denominational courses. This cooperative effort has on the one hand served to promote interdenominational work in leadership education and on the other hand made a distinct contribution to the growing ecumenical movement among the churches.

In the New Standard Curriculum, as modified and approved in 1936, the peak year for number of schools, there were 677 interdenominational schools, with approximately 3,000 classes. About 35,000 credits were issued, and it is safe to say that this indicates an enrollment of not less than 75,000 persons in these community schools. In the same period 120,000 credits were granted by denominational boards using the Standard Curriculum. No accurate check is possible, but indications are that on an average, only from one-third to one-half "take work for credit" in interdenominational schools. The proportion probably runs about the same for most denominational schools, although there is some indication that the proportion of "credit work" may be higher in the denominational schools.

These figures account only for the courses in leadership education which have been completed under the auspices of the International Council and its auxiliaries or under the denominations cooperating in the Standard Curriculum. It does not include the work carried on in Canada under the Religious Education Council of Canada, which maintains its own curriculum of leadership education, similar to that of the International Council of Religious Education. This is composed of five separate divisions of curricula: preparatory, standard, specialization, youth, and advanced. These courses are prepared interdenominationally but are promoted and administered by the denominations. Courses are given in the local church, in cooperative regional schools, in normal schools, in secondary schools, colleges, and theological seminaries, in summer and winter camps, and by correspondence. The Young People's Union of the United Church of Canada has developed Executive Leadership Courses for the officers of various departments. This has resulted in a responsibly trained youth leadership with a very high degree of effectiveness.

The Southern Baptist Convention has also maintained its own plan for leadership education. Through their regular leadership curriculum and through their Baptist Training Unions they have reached hundreds of thousands of their workers. The aggressive outreach of Christian education among Southern Baptists may be attributed in large part to this training program. Perhaps the most arresting aspect of the Southern Baptist program is the high degree of motivation. Large numbers of people pursue many of the courses to completion. The strong emphasis on denominational missions and upon evangelism is a factor, as is also vigorous promotion.

Another leadership education effort of considerable proportion is that of the Evangelical Leadership Training Association. This is a nondenominational program, having its roots in Moody Bible Institute and Scripture Press and appealing for its support to fundamentalist groups of all denominations. It now claims over one hundred accredited schools and has a full-time promotional secretary. It is likely to receive vigorous support from the National Association of Evangelicals. On a community basis it furnishes leadership training opportunities for churches which have not normally cooperated with other cooperative efforts. So far only a little pressure has been put upon denominational boards to recognize work done under the auspices of the Evangelical Leadership Training Association by members of their churches. This pressure may increase as the work of the Association grows.

Various evaluations have been made of the standards provided through the Standard Curriculum of leadership education. At one time there was revolt in many quarters against the whole idea of standards and credits. It seems, however, that there is now a growing appreciation of the value of standardization. It is recognized that an approved standard school is an incentive for better work. Minimum standards, in terms of time and effort, set an ideal for students and are important in motivation of better work.

Yet it must be recognized that there is, as in all education, no magic in the courses themselves to provide good leadership for the church. The Standard Curriculum is only a means. Where this means is used with imagination and skill, it has an effect. Where not so used, it is exceedingly disappointing. It has often been pointed out during recent years that we have not had results in the total program of the local church, or in improved church school practices, commensurate with the time and effort put into the type of leadership education work we have been doing. Many have remarked that there has been precious little carry-over from the average leadership education course into the practice of the teacher. Only a little insight would show us that this might reasonably have been expected. When it comes to methods and techniques, people learn by doing and by participation, by being shown, and not simply by being told.

A great opportunity for leadership education is to be found in the church-related colleges. We are now experiencing the greatest college and university enrollments in the history of American higher education. Church young people as never before are being exposed to rich backgrounds in all the liberal arts and are receiving training in vocational fields.

Religious educators have made comparatively little use of this opportunity to train prospective volunteer lay workers while they are in college. As far back as 1920 a joint committee representing the Council of Church Boards of Education and the Sunday School Council of Evangelical Denominations worked out a program for the offering of a "major" in religious education in church-related colleges. A few denominations made significant use of this program, but the opportunity has never been developed as it might have been.

Practically all strong church-related colleges, together with other privately endowed institutions and some state universities, offer courses in English Bible. Such curricular offerings can be expanded as rapidly as there is a demand for them. Along with the academic teaching must go an unremitting effort to relate the student actively to local church educational programs.

Thus far we have considered the results of the effort to provide the more formal type of leadership education. There are many other ways in which guidance is given to workers in Christian education, and hundreds of thousands of workers are profiting by such efforts. These include numerous conventions and conferences; workshops dealing with specific problems, such as visual aids, the use of the radio, newer types of teaching; an extensive literature on Christian education in the form of books and magazines; guidance for teachers in lesson helps; workers' conferences in the local church; personal counseling on the part of field representatives; missions to teachers. Not the least of these more informal efforts is the extensive effort in the guidance and training of leadership in youth groups, conferences, and camps. If a comparison could be made of the relative effectiveness of the more formal type of leadership courses and these more informal efforts of leadership education, it might well be that in terms of numbers reached and effectiveness, these informal efforts would outstrip the former. There is, however, no point in making such a comparison. Both types of leadership guidance are needed, and the more we can have of both, the better.

V. LOOKING TO THE FUTURE

The task of providing trained leadership for Christian education is so gigantic as to stagger the imagination. A conservative estimate gives the number of workers in Sunday schools alone as two million. To this must be added the very considerable number of persons who are giving leadership in the other agencies of Christian education. It is again estimated, conservatively, that the average life of a church school worker is about three years. In other words, on an average there are 666,666 new workers to be trained every year, to say nothing of the continuing training for those who have gone beyond their first year of service.

The task is also exceedingly difficult. Christian education today is a complex and exacting art. We have already touched upon the difficulty of giving an adequate training to an inexperienced worker who must do his training on such spare time as he can devote to it. To this must be added the difficulty of interesting many of these workers in taking any training at all. It is probably far too optimistic to guess that even one-fourth of all the workers in Christian education ever complete a single course in leadership training, and a large proportion of the remaining ones seldom, if ever, attend the workers' conferences in their own churches or other conferences and conventions through which they might receive a small measure of the guidance they need.[2]

The problem of leadership will not be solved by wishful thinking. We have no reason to believe that a panacea will be found which will cure all the leadership ills. Numerous churches have proved that persistent effort and consecration to a task over a long term will get results. The methods available for leadership training are many. They are sufficiently varied to meet most needs. What is needed is a new consecration of Christian people to the educational work of the church and such devotion to the task that nothing possible will be left undone which will make for more effective Christian education. That is the hope of the future—renewed consecration to the work of Christian teaching and unceasing effort in using the means of training which have been placed at our disposal.

---

[2]In 1943-44, for example, the International Council and its member denominations issued 146,209 leadership education credits. That year the United States churches belonging to the Council reported 1,535,895 Sunday school officers and teachers, or more than ten times the number of credits issued, including those issued to Canadians.

Chapter VII

A Community Approach to Christian Education

*T*HIS chapter will deal with the task of Christian education in a specific geographical area which the churches of that area must do together. It assumes the importance of any church in its own individual work. It recognizes, however, that a total community approach is not possible except by the cooperation of the churches in common effort.

While we shall deal primarily with Christian education, we would not want to give the impression that it is regarded apart from other functions of the church in the community. Christian education is an emphasis in the churches' total strategy. The educational spirit and method should permeate all that the churches do together. In turn, Christian education should itself be permeated by the spirit and method of evangelism, comity, social action and service, and other activities in which the churches together engage.

In this discussion, the *community* is to be understood as a limited geographical area, in which persons and groups are living together, influencing each other, and recognizing certain degrees of interdependence. Its limits are such that people may be in face-to-face relationships. Its existence, boundaries, and nature are determined by various factors: geographical and climatic conditions, transportation facilities, cultural and social traits and contacts, economic services and enterprises, religious and social relationships.

Within the community there may be a few or many neighborhoods—smaller areas in which there is also a community of interest and opportunity for face-to-face relationships. Communities, in turn, will be grouped in larger units, such as a county, a state, a region, a nation, and even the world, having certain characteristics and elements which inspire its citizens to a feeling of "we-ness," which is one of the marks of the community. Yet these larger areas lack certain intimate and vital elements which are common to a genuine community.

The word "community" is also used apart from geographical connotations. We speak, for example, of an association of people based solely on special common interests. The "Christian Rural Fellowship" or the "Protestant community" designate such an association of common interests. But wherever we use the term in that sense we shall endeavor to make clear in the context the special use of the word.

The phrase "social order" also should not be confused with community. Social order designates those patterns of economic, racial, and political relationships which make up the structure and character of social life, particularly the economic and the political. The relationships and the forces which issue from them come to a focus in the community but do not constitute the community.

I. The Spiritual Basis for a Community Approach

That the churches of the community should be concerned with the community life about them is so generally agreed that it should require no defense. There are, nevertheless, those who feel that all such activities on the part of the church are aside from its main business. To all such, let it be said that community concern is rooted in the nature of the Christian faith itself.

1. *The nature of God.*—The basic reason why the churches should be concerned with the community is grounded in the character and purpose of God. God is love. He seeks the good of all through his work as Creator and Redeemer. The most significant force in the universe is the divine good will toward man. God is our Father. All men are made in the image of God. Both the beginning and the ultimate destiny of human life, of individuals and groups, are found in the purpose of their Father in heaven. God's fatherhood makes men brothers. Men are joined to one another as members of the human family under the fatherhood of God. They can realize the potential of their own deepest natures and the promise of their community with other men only as they live in the practical recognition of their spiritual unity. God is within as well as above his world. His will is not fully done at any particular time in history. All social arrangements of which we are a part are judged inadequate, and new paths of community of social living are ever being marked out for us to face.

2. *Man as a social being.*—While each person is unique, at the same time he is also related to other persons. Society is basic to human life. The individual is born into a social group, the family. He partakes of the contribution of the past as well as the present because he is inseparably related to those who have gone before and those who are his contemporaries. The very fact of discovering himself as a person is made possible because there are other persons. Self-consciousness and other-consciousness are two aspects of a single experience.

Man the individual lives and moves in the group. He has no life apart from it. His social world is just as real as the physical universe. He is involved in an economic order. He is part of a society in which there are divisions based on birth, race, creed, and other considerations. He is a citizen of a certain country. There social relationships are facts. The church cannot but be concerned with these facts, because it is concerned with guiding and inspiring man to live these relationships in the light of the gospel which it professes.

3. *Social tension.*—The church is concerned with community life because there is need to resolve the tensions which arise in social living. The community is the focus of dynamic social forces. Within it there are many separate "communities of interest," such as educational, social, religious, cultural, and economic. There are also "communities of opinion," which unite groups of people on broad common agreements but separate them from other groups who hold different opinions.

These tensions require a spiritual ministry for their resolution. Each community requires a body of mutualities sufficient to prevent its social forces from tearing community life apart. This must rest back upon an experience of solidarity which expresses itself in justice, tolerance, and a concern for the common good. It needs also the dynamic force to release and stimulate new energies so that it may develop according to changed conditions and new insights. The members of a community are constantly responding to social and ethical forces which the community exerts upon them. This is a matter of great concern to the churches. Failure to recognize and deal with this fact brings about such contradictions as the disparity between an individual's face-to-face relationships and his business policies and prac-tices. In the first he may be extremely sensitive to the ethical implication of the gospel, while in the second he yields to the authority which the mores of the commu-nity's economic life exert upon him, many of which are based on considerations other than ethical.

The community relationships which he sustains frus-trate the Christian in the practice of his faith at many points. For example, where racial segregation in trans-portation facilities is a matter of law or binding custom, the individual is not as free to practice the Christian insight that men are children of God as he would be if no such law or customs existed. Individual faith and commitment to Christ are independent of any particu-lar form of community organization, but the expression of that faith in justice and brotherhood is very much related to the character of a community.

4. *The church and the community.*—The church as a social institution is involved deeply in the complex life of the community. As in the case of individuals, the community is constantly influencing the church, but it is our faith that the church in turn will also influence the community. The church is included in the community, though its spirit and purpose must transcend it. Granted its concern with the salvation of the individual, the church cannot deal with the great issues of evil, sin, and guilt with anything less than a gospel that is as true to the insights of community as it is to the insights of the individual life.

The church is one of many institutions in the commu-nity which are struggling for position and seeking to make their faith and insight felt in community life. We are concerned with the church's approach to the community just because we do believe that the church has a message and program which have the power to win the ascendancy in any community. Community life is amenable to change, in both its character and influence. History shows that such changes wait only upon time. Public opinion does change, and consequently also public behavior.

5. *A Protestant strategy.*—These considerations lead to the question of how the church may properly proceed to make its impact upon community life. The position here assumed will underlie the more practical suggestions which follow in the rest of this chapter.

American government was founded on certain religious presuppositions. Many believe that its existence and preservation depend on a continuing undergirding by a vital religious faith. It will readily be granted that the churches of the community have a responsibility for relating these basic concepts of freedom and democracy to the ongoing process of community life.

But what of the church and politics? All too often it is assumed that politics is inherently evil and that somehow Christians soil themselves by participating in it. As a matter of fact, politics is the science and art of government. Politics is good or bad as people make it. Christians make politics the means by which community life may be realized.

For the Protestant church, the end of political activity is not to gain some special privilege or power for the church, but the spiritual, moral, and social welfare of the community as a whole. To achieve this end, it is neither desirable nor necessary for the church to act in any other capacity than as a moral force in the community. It addresses itself to those in public office concerning their duties as the duly constituted representatives of the people in the formation and administration of government policy. Whenever its members come into public office, it holds that they should be directed, not by the authority of the church, but by their own enlightened and informed Christian consciences.

However, the fact that Protestantism rejects the idea of the church as an organized political force does not negate the obligation of the church to express in appropriate ways its social concern and to make its influence felt in political life. Some of the avenues through which the church may serve as an instrument for social change through political action, without itself becoming a political party, include the following:

a) The members of the churches are themselves citizens and therefore have not only the obligation but also the opportunity to express their Christianity through their citizenship. Christian living has in it the obligation to use citizenship as a part of one's service to the Kingdom of God on earth.

b) The Christian church has the responsibility for informing and training its members in awareness and understanding of appropriate action on social needs and issues in the light of Christian principles. This responsibility should be not merely "another" element in the educational program of the churches but central to it.

c) As the church proceeds with its program of social education and action, divisions of opinion will inevitably arise. A local congregation, a national body, or an intermediate group should use such occasions as opportunities to engage their members in a search for relevant facts and interpretations that may lead to a discovery of Christian courses of action. When, at the end of such a process, division still prevails, it is the church's responsibility to indicate whatever common ground exists and what differences remain unresolved. Christians should be urged to act according to their Christian consciences. In its public utterances the church should state frankly the range of significant agreements and disagreements, indicating where possible the proportions of each.

d) There will be other occasions when the church at various points in its official life will have achieved virtual unanimity about the Christian position which should be taken on specific issues deemed to have religious and moral significance. When this happens the church has both a right and an obligation to make its witness known and to take steps to make that witness effective.

e) The individual Christian should be encouraged to associate himself with voluntary groups, both within and without the churches, which are formed around convictions on issues considered vital to social well-being. When the individual Christian does this in relation to nonchurch groups in particular, he should use discriminating judgment, not only as to the ends sought by the groups, but as to methods used to achieve those ends. At the same time, he should exercise his judgment in such a way as not necessarily to inhibit him from participation with such groups because they are not equally in line with Christian insights at all points. Of special importance is it that the Christian church encourage groups within the fellowship to unite on behalf of special concerns and interests. Thus they may grow through such discipline and provide leadership for their fellow members.

f) The role of the church in a ministry of reconciliation, when combined with a passion for justice based upon love and brotherhood, is of great importance. It will often happen that God's judgment seems to rest more heavily upon one group than upon another. However, the church as such will remember that all parties to a conflict have sinned and fallen short of the will of God, and that its ultimate task is to bring all parties in conflict to a higher understanding of their relationship to one another as children of God. The church's function, conceived in such reconciling terms, gives it a creative and redemptive role in community life which no other institution is equipped to perform.

g) It is also important to organize Christians into vocational groups for the purpose of studying the implications of Christianity for the practice of their vocations. The responsibilities of investors and consumers should be studied in the same way; so also executives and labor. The possibilities of such group inquiry and action resulting therefrom are great. By neglecting this aspect of adult Christian education, the churches are missing an excellent opportunity to bring the Christian testimony to bear upon a secular social order.

h) In all of this it is imperative that the church make its own life and practice a demonstration of the Christian ethic. As the church puts into operation in its corporate life its own highest ideals in interracial relations, in economic practices, including the investment of its funds, and in other phases of its own life, it makes its strongest impact upon the community.

II. The Community as Educator

Powerful educative forces issue from the complex of human relationships which is the community. These the churches must take into account as they plan their total educational program. The community provides the setting in which Christian education is carried on, but it is also itself a teacher.

Studies in how character grows have emphasized the crucial importance of the relationships people have with one another. These relationships include many kinds of situations and responses to a great variety of persons and groups. What happens to an individual, and what he does as a result of these relationships with his friends, the janitor, the corner policeman, the neighborhood grocer, his teachers and parents, makes up his total educational experience. It is the involvement of persons in a complex pattern of relationships, which is the essence of community life, that has such powerful educational influence, whether for good or for evil. We have seen earlier that this whole complex of experience is the curriculum of Christian education in the broadest sense.

If it be said that such community impacts are indirect, incidental, and relatively unplanned for educational influences, the statement must be accepted as essentially true. But this does not mean that their educational force and value are any less important or effective. They are probably more so. This poses for us our most distressing educational problem: how to devise a positive program which will utilize, redirect, or counteract, as may be necessary, this community influence to make it less harmful or more useful. The community teaches willy-nilly. As Christian educators we endeavor to see to it that it is made an influence for desirable character growth. Our problem may be sharpened by looking at it from three points of view.

First, let us look at our American communities: large cities, towns, and rural areas. The following questions which may be raised about them indicate the many ways in which the dominant characteristics of a community may shape the character of its citizens:

1. Its main economic interests and the way they are carried on: Are they industry, commerce, farming, a race track, or a divorce mill?

2. Its leading citizens: Who are they, and is their moral leadership constructive?

3. The community agencies which are prominently brought to public attention: Are they predominantly selfish or social in their purposes?

4. Its degree of solidarity, of unity, of mutual friendliness: Are there many conflicts which repeatedly divide the population into factions and classes, or have the citizens learned to work and live together?

5. The extent to which there is an emphasis upon cultural plans and agencies—schools, churches, libraries, and the like: Are these institutions the pride and joy of its people, or do the citizens think mainly in terms of commercial enterprises and profits therefrom?

6. The physical layout and plan for the community: To what extent is it a place of beauty, of order, and of comfort for all the people?

7. The motives for recreation in the community: Is recreation provided primarily for profit by commercial agencies without regard to character outcomes, or is it

furnished by socially minded agencies for the character growth of the participants?

8. The general mores of the community: What is its standard of recreation? Its attitude toward honesty and sex morality? Its regard for law and order? Its attitude on gambling?

Next, let us view the problem from the standpoint of certain types of communities. There are some communities which place intolerable handicaps upon the churches and the forces of Christian education by the very nature of their organized and communal life. In such communities, no matter how hard churches attempt to lead their people into the Christian life, the community influences work, not with, but against, them. Consider, for example, the following types:

1. The new "mushroom" type. The war emergency areas and special housing projects for veterans are fresh in our thinking, but they are not the first, nor are they likely to be the last, of this kind.

2. The old, gone-to-seed, inbred communities from which the young and ambitious persons have gone out to find better opportunities.

3. The "half-and-half" communities, outwardly respectable but for various reasons tolerating some situation or practice, economic or political, which is destructive of character.

4. The communities which may be said to be indifferent, having little or no interest or pride in matters cultural or spiritual.

5. The type of community whose physical location and structure are handicaps to easy transportation, to beautification, and to good health.

6. The community in which antagonisms between racial, religious, and cultural groups have become so strong that restrictive covenants, bitter political conflicts, discrimination in education and employment, and other manifestations of social cleavage are common practices.

7. The communities in which the major industry is positively harmful or at least questionable, so far as its influence on character is concerned.

Finally, let us consider one emergent factor which is affecting the life of almost all communities, which may prove to be of tremendous importance in the next few decades. It is becoming increasingly difficult to maintain Sunday as a day on which a major portion of the task of propagating religion through worship, preaching, and teaching can be accomplished. Increased travel has led us to become a much more mobile people than was formerly the case. With Saturday or Monday almost a universal holiday, and with a forty-hour week an actuality, and a thirty-hour week a possibility, the week-end vacation is becoming almost an American behavior pattern.

Rural as well as urban areas will feel the effect of this new development, although in a different way. The result is that the church is faced with a sociological trend from which there is no escape—the likelihood of finding many of its constituency away from home and on the move from Friday to Monday.

This changing community pattern demands that we find the best new ways for evangelizing both the church-minded citizens and the larger unreached multitude. Whatever the particular plans evolved, however, there is one imperative which must be considered: a single local church or a single denomination working alone cannot in any appreciable degree act effectively. The problem is both so vast and of such a nature that collective or corporate action is required. Our churches must pool their resources in this day of new problems and new procedures. Only so can the quality of educational and spiritual environment be kept high and the community be worthy of the title of Teacher of the Worthy Life.

III. Imperatives for Interchurch Cooperation

These considerations of the nature of the community and its inevitable educational influence make it imperative that the churches of the community work together in devising and promoting an effort in Christian education which is adequate to the need. The imperatives which lead to this conclusion may be summarized in the following propositions:

1. The gospel which the Christian church proclaims is a unity of faith and life. The program of Christian education which seeks to further the acceptance and practice of the gospel in the community should itself be a witness to this unity. In turn, such a demonstration of unity becomes a new factor in a program of education for unity.

2. The Christian ethic is one in which the strong share their strength with the weak. All churches have both their strength and their weakness in comparison with others, so that all need the pooling of resources, material and spiritual, that comes through cooperative effort.

3. Each community needs a core of cohesiveness. Through lack of unity among themselves, the Christian churches can be a divisive instead of a cohesive force. When this occurs the churches are not only undermining

a prerequisite of community life, but they are betraying religion, which is the ultimate unifying power in human life, both individual and corporate.

4. Each local community is made up of diverse social groups—economic, cultural, racial, etc. These are found in varying degrees in the local churches of the community, depending often upon their location and their denominational affiliation. Interchurch cooperation in Christian education will more adequately deal with the needs which arise out of this diversity because it represents the whole community, which itself is socially inclusive.

5. The individual member of the local church lives his life not only as a member of a parish but as a citizen of the community of which his parish is but a part. If his local church is to aid him in meeting his religious responsibilities and opportunities arising from his community relationships, the church itself will be strengthened by sharing in interchurch cooperation.

6. The local community is a part of the national and world-wide community, and if it is to rise both to its needs and its responsibilities it must think and act accordingly. Of all the groups and institutions in the local community, the church is potentially most capable of meeting these needs and responsibilities because of its universal faith and its world outreach. Interchurch cooperation is indispensable for interpreting fully the meaning of world Christianity to the community.

7. The local community, both as a whole and in each of its parts, is an educational force. If the churches are to be a vital element in determining the character of that force, there must be conscious planning and effort

on the community level by the churches in their own Christian education program. The several interests in the community that are devoted to education and character building are themselves organized on the community level. The Christian education forces of the community will be better equipped to work with and through such groups if their approach is likewise community wide.

IV. THE EDUCATIONAL TASKS OF THE CHURCHES WORKING TOGETHER

The educational work of the churches in a community, whether viewed individually or as an interchurch task, is one program. From both points of view it is concerned with the welfare of individuals and of the community as a whole. The local church establishes and maintains a direct relationship with individuals through teaching, worship, fellowship, and service. It prepares individuals for influence and leadership in social living. On the other hand, the interchurch program deals with the needs of the community as a whole. It constitutes a channel through which the Christian concern for social living finds expression in community life. These two approaches complement each other and are essentially one. The collective or corporate functions of the churches in the community must be firmly anchored in the life and work of the individual churches, which in turn are dependent upon interchurch action for the effective expression of their ideals and purposes in the corporate life of the community.

This essential character of interchurch activity must be realized by denominations as well as by the local churches before cooperative effort can approach its necessary effectiveness. Interchurch councils are as indispensable to the denominations for winning community life for Christ as their foreign missions societies are for the winning of other nations. Their work is determined by the same comprehensive Christian strategy which underlies the imperative of foreign missions, and they deserve to have the support which corresponds to their importance.

The areas of possible cooperation in the interest of Christian education are many and vary from community to community. For any community these possible activities must be examined and re-examined until a group of clearly defined functions for that community emerges, satisfactory to its local church and denominational leadership. The following outline is offered as a tentative analysis of the possible fields of cooperation:

1. *Community-wide fellowship and sharing of experience.*—The sense of Christian comradeship in a common task and the sharing of experiences in a community-wide program of Christian education are sources of spiritual undergirding for the Christian cause when they arise out of facing the common needs of life in the community. The interchurch council itself, with its regular and special activities of planning and action, will be a primary source of fellowship and sharing. Examples of common activities toward this end are: annual community-wide conferences and conventions, superintendents' and age-group workers' fellowships, youth councils, young adult fellowships, ministers' associations.

2. *Ecumenical education.*—The actual experience of respecting and sharing the Christian faith in interchurch activities is a most productive kind of ecumenical education, but this must be definitely planned for. Inter-

church councils must stimulate a sense of belonging to the church universal. This may be done through well-planned services of worship which emphasize the universal nature of the Christian fellowship, regular opportunities for special ecumenical studies, and leadership in integrating this emphasis into each local church program.

3. *Active concern in the churches and in the community for public education.*—The challenge of secular trends in public education makes it urgent that the churches and synagogues engage in bold experimentation with new patterns of relationships between the public schools and the churches of a local community. The goals, objectives, and needs of public schools need to be interpreted to the churches, and the functional values of religion need to be interpreted to public school teachers and administrators. This may lead to conferences of churchmen and public school teachers, principals, and superintendents, for fellowship and mutual understanding; an annual occasion for welcoming new teachers, for deepening the sense of Christian vocation among teachers, and for appreciation of faithful service; conferences for developing understanding of the problems faced by public schools and support of measures for improvement of public school equipment and leadership; cultivation of closer relations between interchurch councils and teachers' colleges, accrediting agencies, and professional associations; support of the commendable activities of public schools; encouragement of high moral standards; observance of American Education Week; the use of criticism only as a last resort.

4. *Developing public opinion favorable to religious education.*—The importance of public opinion increases

as social organizations become more complex and inter-related. The purpose and function of religious education and its relation to the problems of community life must be continually brought to the attention of the people. A sustained effort to create a favorable public opinion is a central function of interchurch councils. This suggests effective relations with public opinion forming forces, such as the press, radio, and motion pictures; the use of special days or weeks, such as Religious Education Week, National Family Week; recognition of special meritorious service by leaders in religious education.

5. *Cooperative efforts to reach all the people with religious education.*—The churches of a local community need the strength of one another to reach all the people for which they have responsibility. Through these efforts the churches will extend their outreach to people not now reached by individual local churches, increase the religious education of their own people, and permeate the community with an appreciation of Christian values. Examples of specific effort to meet this community need are: community surveys, community-wide emphases through Religious Education Week and other opportunities, vacation and weekday church schools, radio education.

6. *Community coordinating councils of character-building agencies.*—The churches should be leaders in the support of movements designed to coordinate the character-building agencies of the community. They should encourage them, use them, and provide leadership as well as specialized skills to help them realize their fullest potentialities for character development.

7. *Educational undergirding for effective community social action.*—The educational functions of the churches in community social problems are widely accepted in Protestantism, however much difference of opinion there may be about other phases of Christian social action. The educational forces have a large responsibility as well as opportunity, therefore, to make education a vital factor in community social relations. This can be done best, perhaps, through a program of Christian citizenship enlistment and training based on specific factual data regarding the community's own organization and needs. In so far as possible it should issue in action on civic matters. As with all other basic functions of the churches, education for Christian citizenship must be grounded in the local churches, but it must have a community outreach which finds expression through interchurch councils.

New patterns of local interchurch program planning, curriculum development, and integration of local church objectives with cooperative effort must be found if Protestant Christianity is to make effective in community life its inner social convictions and idealism. Some activities in this field might be: a school of social relations or Christian citizenship, an annual recognition service for young people who reach voting age, correlation of church programs with social studies in public schools, research and survey into community problems, specific action projects designed to change social conditions, inclusion of minority racial and national groups into a community-wide Christian fellowship of love and concern, acquainting people with proposed social legislation and its religious implications, and providing for representation of the churches at legislative hearings.

8. *Religious education needs of public or private institutions for care of unfortunate people.*—Dependents and delinquent children, the chronically ill, the mentally ill, the aged, the handicapped, those in prison, are often overlooked. Including adult criminals, there are estimated to be more than a million and a half persons in the hospitals, homes, correctional and other institutions of the United States at any one time, exclusive of those who might be in an institution for only a day or two. The service needed is highly skilled, but, in consultation with the authorities in charge of the institutions, and under the guidance of experts in these matters, the churches of a local community can render valuable service.

9. *Collective self-service activities to strengthen the religious education programs of the local churches themselves.*—This area provides the largest possibility for conflict between denominations and interchurch councils. Service to local churches has been increasingly recognized to be primarily a denominational responsibility as the denominations' programs of Christian education have steadily increased. Such services therefore need to be planned with full knowledge of the program of each denomination for its local churches, and in close collaboration with denominational leaders.

However, the idea of the churches in a community helping each other and sharing the cost of services which meet the needs of all is fundamentally sound. Many churches never receive the help of denominational field-workers because of the latters' inability to reach them all. New patterns of relationships and programs must be sought through courageous experimentation if the needs of thousands of local churches in America for Christian education leadership are to be met.

Common types of activity in this field are: schools of Christian living; community leadership schools, conferences, and institutes; cooperative laboratory schools; employment of a community director of Christian education for service directly to local churches; and perhaps the development of community buildings for religious education and recreation.

A vexing problem for many churches arises from their small numbers and poor equipment, due to competition for constituency with other churches. They cannot grade closely, cannot get the necessary leadership, and find it hard to build the morale for a good church school. It would seem that the time has come when this problem might be solved in many communities by cooperative effort in the holding of a Sunday school and youth group, as is now often the case with weekday and vacation church schools. Such cooperative effort would be to the immense gain of each church concerned, but most important of all, to the cause of Christ in the community.

V. COMMUNITY ORGANIZATION FOR CHRISTIAN EDUCATION

A fairly standardized pattern of interchurch organization for the community has emerged. This is the council of churches. It is inclusive of all the church interests, such as comity, social service and action, joint special-day services, united every-member canvasses, as well as Christian education. It is officially representative of the churches, either through duly elected delegates of member local churches, or through denominational delegates representing the local churches of each denomination affiliated with the council.

These councils of churches are usually successors to earlier community organizations, such as Sunday school associations, ministerial associations, or other less inclusive efforts at cooperation. In some communities the cooperative effort is still limited to Christian education, leadership training, ministers' meetings, weekday religious education, or some similar specific function.

In the inclusive council of churches, Christian education must find a place among other activities, commensurate with its importance. The problem involved here is similar to that of its place in the total program of the local church. The following positions have been fairly well established through experience:

1. Christian education is more likely to benefit than to lose by an inclusive council of churches community organization. Granting the advantages of promoting a specific interest, it is nevertheless true that Christian education is so closely related to all phases of the church's work that any plan setting it off by itself would be illogical. If it sometimes happens that Christian education is relegated to a minor place, as in many local churches, that is a risk which must be taken.

2. Provision should be made for the representatives from local churches to the council of churches to include one or more who have a major interest in Christian education. Thus may reasonable assurance be given that this interest will receive adequate attention in program and budget.

3. Representation of Christian education within the structure of the council may be by one of two plans. The first and more common plan is to have a general committee on Christian education, with subcommittees

for its specific phases of work such as leadership, children's work, youth work, vacation church schools. This facilitates the coordination of the several educational activities and gives Christian education a strong visible place in the council program. The second plan is to have separate committees on the several aspects of work in Christian education, such as those named earlier in the paragraph, coordinate with committees on comity, social action, evangelism. Those favoring this plan maintain that it is more likely to permeate the whole work of the council with the spirit and method of Christian education than the first.

4. The council should be competent and willing to cooperate with other religious groups in the community so as to present a united front to irreligion. This is especially important in its work with children and young people. The Protestant council will, therefore, maintain cordial relationships with Catholic and Jewish groups in the development of such projects as weekday church schools, Religious Education Week, religious education for citizenship. This cooperation should be based upon common interests, with a full understanding that major differences still exist and will still motivate each group toward the propagation of its own faith.

5. Similarly, the council should effectively relate the churches to other character-building agencies of the community. The services of such agencies will thus be made available to the churches, and the contributions of religion may be made available to the agencies.[1]

---

[1]Detailed suggestions for the organization of a community interchurch council are to be found in pamphlet No. 2 in the Church Cooperation Series, prepared by the Inter-Council Field Department and entitled ''How to Organize a Council of Churches and Religious Education.''

VI. Religion and Public Education

We have already considered the corporate responsibility of the churches of the community for the welfare of public education. There is a phase of that matter which deserves more extended examination. It is the place of religion in public education.

Religion held an important place in early American education. Through the years there has been a gradual but sure elimination of the religious element. This has been deemed necessary in order to have common schools for the children of all faiths and no faith. In support of this policy there has been frequent reference to the doctrine of "the separation of church and state."

In our day there is a marked desire on the part of many, both schoolmen and churchmen, to re-examine this trend toward secularization and its evident results. It has been questioned whether a school which avoids the controversial problem of religion by being neutral on it has, in fact, a neutral effect. There has been an expansion of the school program to make it more and more an expression of total community interest and concern. It is rightly questioned whether in such a school the omission of religion does not in fact have a negative effect.

Moreover, a school which seeks to be a fair interpreter of the culture and life of a community can scarcely maintain that it succeeds in this if it makes little or no reference to the expressions of religious interest and activity which are abundant in every community.

To furnish an intelligent understanding of the place of religion in human history and in contemporary life is part of the function of general education. Religion is not a piece of life that can be isolated for study but an aspect of individual and social experience in its totality. Every educational discipline should take account of the religious elements that enter into the area of experience which it undertakes to explore.

The sacred doctrine of separation of church and state has itself been brought into question at the point of its common interpretation. Does it necessarily mean complete independence of one from the other? We know that it does not, because the church is subject to the laws of the state and enjoys its privileges, such as freedom from taxation. We know also that the state was founded on certain fundamental religious assumptions and that the state avails itself of the ministry of religion at many points. What the principle does mean is that the freedom and responsibility of each should be assured. Neither one should be allowed to control the other. This applies to worship, religious education, or any other activity which the churches claim as exclusively their own. On the other hand, the state must be free of domination or control by ecclesiastical organizations.

Applied to education, this would mean that the school may confront all its pupils with a fair recognition of the existence and meaning of religion and religious institutions, put them in possession of an objective body of facts on the basis of which intelligent individual judgments may be made, and predispose them to give a fair and impartial consideration to the claims of religion on the loyalties of men. It may not offer sectarian instruction in religion or seek a decision for any particular religious point of view. Just as surely should it prevent the unbelieving teacher from pressing his claims on his pupils by refutation or ridicule of the religious point of view.

When classes in religion are held under the auspices of the churches on released time, the school has an obligation to require that it be done under conditions which will assure an educative experience to justify the time released, but it may not prescribe the content of what is to be taught.

Education at its best is an expression of the life and interests of the entire community. Every community may have the kind of schools it wants, and no community can evade its responsibility for its schools. It follows that the religious interests of the community have a right to an expression in education and that the churches of the community, representing as they do the organization of the religious forces, should be looked to for making this claim articulate. Let it be said emphatically, however, that this does not mean that the churches are asking the schools to do their work for them. As here conceived, the place of religion in public education is a concern of the entire community, and the lack of it prevents education from fulfilling its true and whole obligation. Therefore, this is a task for the schools.

A measure of acceptance of this responsibility for religious education is found in the weekday church school movement. In many communities this is supported by the schoolmen as well as by the church leaders. It recognizes the right of the school to devote a part of the school day to the teaching of religion, in cooperation with the religious institutions of the community. An evaluation of this movement has been made in Chapters III and IV. The only question we shall raise here is whether it constitutes an answer to the problem of religion in public education. The weekday school does not offer a complete answer to this problem, because (1) it still maintains a separateness for religion from general education, whereas what we are contending for is that education should be a unitary process; (2) the possible time available is insufficient; (3) it separates pupils into sectarian groups, thus making a common religious education for all impossible; (4) it may not include those children whose parents are opposed or indifferent to religion, and thus prevent a fair exposure on their part to the necessary understanding if a competent judgment is to be made; (5) it can make no provision for the utilization of the spiritual and religious values in all the school subjects, which, as we shall see, are the chief vehicles for an understanding of religion as it may be taught in the public school.

We would maintain therefore that the public school has a responsibility for education in religion which goes beyond its cooperation with churches and synagogues by dismissing pupils to them. Nothing short of the inclusion of religion in the curriculum of the public school will suffice. But how is this to be done where there are so many sectarian viewpoints and some who reject all religion? The principle to be followed is that such education must be unsectarian, unbiased, and free of all partisan pressure. Under these conditions, we believe that the problem can be solved, though in practice it will require a great deal of further experimentation.

There are some who feel that the solution lies in the inclusion in the regular school program, under school auspices, of a "core" of religious instruction based on the common elements in the major faiths. We consider this plan to have doubtful value. It means, in effect, that the school shall adopt an eclectic theology, built upon the beliefs that Protestants, Catholics, and Jews hold in common. This could hardly be satisfactory to anyone. There are, of course, cities, towns, and rural districts in America which are so nearly homogeneous religiously that a body of Protestant or Catholic or Jewish doctrine could, with public approval, be taught as the true faith. In some communities it is apparently being done. Furthermore, the principle of local control to which we subscribe opens the way to doctrinal instruction in religion where legal questions are not raised. But the danger to religious freedom involved in it is too obvious to be ignored. Most Protestants believe in the right of the citizen to unbelief as well as to belief. If the school commits itself to a body of religious doctrine, that negative right is in danger of being overridden.

It is our contention that the teaching of religion does not need to be limited to commonly accepted elements, provided such teaching is done under the well-established principles which apply to all subjects on which there is division of opinion. Such subject matter must be studied with integrity and with complete fidelity to the principle of free inquiry. The fact that religion holds an exalted place in our thought and life must not be made the ground of a claim that it is privileged subject matter with respect to objective inquiry. This need hamper the study of a religious classic no more than it hampers the study of the Declaration of Independence or the Mayflower Compact, which contain profound religious affirmations. Nor need the requirement of free and honest inquiry be a limitation in the study of religious institutions any more than in the study of political and economic groups with their sharply conflicting philosophies. Here, as always, respect for persons and for freedom of conscience is of the essence. Where it obtains, education can proceed unhampered. Where it is lacking, no education worthy of the name is possible.

It is in order to give a few concrete examples of how this plan might be worked out in practice. The study of literature, whether in formal classes, or in relation to informal projects, should include our major religious classic, the Bible. From any point of view, the Bible must be considered a basic contribution to our literary heritage. To be ignorant of it is to be less than culturally literate. The study of it need involve no more sectarian indoctrination than the study of Milton or Dante, Shakespeare or Tennyson, provided there is brought to it the same reverence for creative work that all literary study demands.

Likewise, the study of contemporary community life should include the religious institutions, as well as those of government, industry, and social welfare. There is ample evidence that this can be done as part of the social studies program without untoward results and with educational effectiveness.

But how shall teachers be provided for this type of religious teaching? It is a part of the professional preparation of a teacher to achieve competence in the handling of the religious elements of his particular discipline. This is important in almost every field but indispensable in the humanities, the arts, and the social sciences. This does not mean specialization any more than adequate attention to reading ability or physical and mental hygiene on the part of every teacher involves specialization. It does mean that competence in most fields of education requires an intelligent grasp of the way in which man's religious outlook and concern have entered into his cultural development.

The public school has a responsibility to develop as far as it can the spiritual implications of its own common life. It owes an obligation to the community's religious forces to lift its direct and indirect teaching above the level of materialism or thoughtless sensory gratification. It can assume a much larger responsibility than it has usually undertaken for the creation and nurture of spiritual values. Respect for personality; high moral standards of conduct; love of truth, goodness, and beauty; wonder and reverence before a vast and mysterious universe; and responsible use of freedom—these and many more must be objects of the school's serious and sustained concern.

A question inevitably arises concerning the use of forms and symbols of worship in the schools. Simple services of worship are very commonly a feature of school assembly programs. During the observance of the great Christian festivals the use of religious symbolism in the schools is widespread. Such practices are sometimes criticized, but in general they seem to have effective sanction. Although from one point of view worship involves a closer identification with religion than the study of religious beliefs, it seems to be generally assumed that simple services of Christian worship in the public schools, including the reading of Scripture, do no violence to the principle of separation of church and state. On the other hand, in communities that are sharply divided in religious allegiance, consideration may well be given to the possibility of developing forms of worship that are meaningful to members of different faiths. Even the minimum of such expression—a ritual of silence—may be productive of a deeply reverent mood. In the interest of religious freedom Protestants are bound to sustain the right of withdrawal on grounds of conscience from any class or activity that an individual pupil or his parents regard as harmful to his religious life. This is a principle to be observed with all strictness and, in general, any doubt as to the validity of the objection should be resolved in favor of the objector. Not only so, but the school has a positive responsibility in all such cases to secure to the child immunity from social pressure or censure.

We should note that there is a difference between the function of the school and that of the church and the home in the teaching of religion. Those who contend that the public school cannot "teach" religion are right to the extent that teaching implies the induction of youth into a particular religious body with a distinctive form of worship and way of life. In a sense, the public school, as many people insist, can teach only "about" religion. But knowledge begins with acquaintance—with knowledge "about." With that necessary preparation carefully made, the home and church can go on with their further work of more intensive religious education.

Our main criticism of the secular educational system is that it results in religious illiteracy, leaving a void which makes the task of intensive religious education difficult, if not impossible. General education should build a foundation in awareness and sensitivity upon which growing persons may build as their own free choice directs. Just as an adequate social education lays a foundation for organized political activity in accord with free choice, so it should equip youth for making intelligent judgments with reference to religious activities.

The school will come to a point beyond which it cannot go, and at which the churches must step in with what they consider fuller Christian truth. It is the obligation of the school to leave the way open for such further development by religious institutions, not to present a "closed system" of moral or spiritual interpretation with none other than human and finite references. It is the obligation of the church to support this cultivation of spiritual values as a new ally in religious teaching by means of which all children will be helped to rise above what otherwise might be a crass materialism, and those children reached by more specific religious education will respond more quickly and generously to the fuller teaching of the gospel.

It should be understood that there is a division of labor here. It is the obligation of the church so to understand its faith that it will assume its own task of instruction, meanwhile welcoming the school's assistance in helping children and youth live that faith in the classroom, on the playground, and at the prom. The church should welcome gratefully as an ally any institution which aids in character development, building upon such foundations the greater structure of Christian personality.

VII. The Churches and Community Agencies of Informal Education

Almost every American community has one or more agencies of recreation and informal education seeking to serve the people of that community. In 1937 the

American Youth Commission listed over 200 national agencies serving youth, and there are similarly large numbers serving children and adults. Some of these are privately supported, while others are tax-supported in whole or in part. During the war there was a tendency to increase services of this kind.

There is ample evidence that the way in which children, youth, and adults spend their leisure time is one of the most determinative of all character-forming influences. At certain stages of development, the club or scout troop to which a youth belongs may be more influential in molding attitudes and habits than the school, the church, or even the home. Especially is this true when children spend weeks or months in summer camps. The Rotary Club may be a more effective educational institution than all the adult Bible classes of a town.

Granting the contribution of these agencies and the concern of the churches for the total educational impact of the community, it is imperative that the churches of the community take account of the work of these agencies and relate themselves to it. Gradually a larger measure of coordination is being achieved among these agencies themselves. Through the Recreation or Group Work Section of Councils of Social Agencies, common interests are discussed, resources of leadership are sometimes shared, and cooperative undertakings are carried out. A larger measure of coordination on the national level is developing through the formation in 1943 of the Associated Youth Serving Organizations (AYSO).

Little progress has been made, however, in relating the churches to these interagency councils. Although many individual churches maintain cordial relationships in one way or another with the Scouts, the "Y," or some other agency, patterns of cooperation between councils of churches and councils of other community agencies have seldom been worked out. In other words, the procedure thus far has been largely piecemeal. A statesmanlike approach to this problem of coordination on the part of both churches and agencies is clearly called for and mutually desired.

Basic to any move toward further coordination of effort is an analysis of the specific points where the churches have a concern about the program of these leisure-time agencies and where their potential contributions may best be made.

1. The churches should be concerned that these agencies achieve maximum effectiveness in developing character and personality in accordance with Christian standards. These values are sought both for the large numbers of those not otherwise reached by the churches and for those actively related to the church. It is important for the sake of the integration of the experience of youth that churches and recreational agencies work toward common ends of personal development and social reconstruction.

2. The churches should be concerned that all of their young people shall have the experience of participation in one or more of the leisure-time agencies of the community. Although there is need to guard against undue competition of agencies for the time of youth outside of school and church hours, there is even greater need for the extension of these recreational services to a larger proportion of the youth of our communities. Studies show that one-half or more of the children and

youth of the average community take no active part in any organized recreational or educational program outside of the school. Participation of church youth in leisure-time programs apart from church auspices takes on added significance when opportunities are provided for interdenominational, interfaith, and interracial experiences.

3. The churches are concerned about better utilization of the techniques and program resources of these recreational agencies to be made available in one of two ways: (1) through a troop, club, or other unit attached directly to the church; (2) by soliciting the aid of an agency leader in developing the churches' program with youth.

4. The churches have a concern to help supply and train leaders for community organizations, both public and private. There is no more effective way for the churches to make their contribution to the development of persons in leisure-time activities than through the devoted service of laymen as board members and volunteer leaders in these agencies.

5. In communities where no adequate coordination of recreational agencies has been achieved, the churches may be in a position to take the lead in bringing them together. This does not mean official sponsorship or control on the part of the churches but a responsibility for seeing that sound principles are followed in interagency organization.

Patterns for cooperation between the churches as a body and other community agencies are so undeveloped that we can only suggest principles for exploration and experimentation.

It is important to distinguish carefully the varying aims, approaches, and organizational practices of these community groups. There is as great variety in this respect among these agencies as among denominations. Churchmen who are seriously interested in church-agency cooperation need to make a study of the philosophy and program of the major agencies.

For example, a different type of cooperation on the part of churches must be worked out with those agencies that do not operate through building centers of their own but carry on their work in decentralized fashion in the community. Again, some of these agencies avoid any direct religious instruction or affiliation, whereas others have an avowed religious purpose and seek definite affiliation with the churches. Methods of work differ, also: some stress the formation of small, closely knit groups; others put the emphasis on mass recreational activities or individual participation according to interests. Again, some of these agencies are local in constituency and control; others are nation wide in scope and have a more or less uniform program to establish.

1. The first step in community coordination probably is an interchange of experiences among leaders of the churches and the agencies for the sake of more accurate information and mutual understanding.

2. Community-wide patterns of coordination should take into account successful experiences of cooperation already gained on a more limited scale. In a number of communities, for example, councils dealing with recreation for teen-age youth have been functioning with representation from the churches, the "Y's," and other agencies. The experience of local interchurch youth

councils warrants special study, as do also coordinating councils in smaller communities.

3. Such exploration should lead to experimentation in church-agency coordination in a few communities of different sizes and types. The main purpose of such efforts should be: (*a*) to work out basic principles to guide individual churches and agencies as they seek closer cooperation; (*b*) to undertake a limited number of cooperative projects, such as a joint undertaking in the recruiting and training of volunteer leaders, or a coordinated approach to sections of the community where the recreational and religious resources for youth are wholly inadequate.

Chapter VIII

Agencies for Promotion and Supervision

*T*HE subcommittee of the Committee on the Study of Christian Education which dealt with the agencies for the promotion and supervision of Christian education gave its attention primarily to the structure and functions of the International Council of Religious Education. Some of their findings are embodied in this chapter, but much of their work dealt with technical problems of no great interest to the general reader. This chapter has been expanded considerably beyond the report in order to round out the treatment of the agencies for promotion and supervision, with special reference to problems affecting the local church.

From the early days of the Sunday school, Christian leaders have been interested in promoting the use of this instrument of Christian education and the improvement of its work. As new means of Christian education have been developed, these, too, have gathered to themselves their own promotional agencies. As they mature, they tend to come into the general movement of Christian education and to come under the established promotional and supervisory organization.

Considering the fact that the Sunday school was initially a laymen's movement, it was only natural that the first of these organizations should be nondenominational and nonecclesiastical in character. Considering its growth and popularity, it was also natural that the denominational organizations should want to incorporate it as one of their interests and responsibilities. These two approaches—nondenominational or interdenominational and denominational—have existed side by side through nearly a century and a quarter, at times vying with each other for mastery, but more and more accepting the position that an essential contribution is to be made by each approach and progressively achieving a synthesis of effort through cooperative relationships.

I. NONDENOMINATIONAL AGENCIES

1. *Sunday school unions.*—Robert Raikes himself was influential in the establishment of the first of these promotional agencies. This was in 1785, only five years after the organization of his first Sunday school in Gloucester, and was called the Sunday School Society. Its purpose was "to establish and support Sunday schools in the Kingdom of Great Britain." In America it was Philadelphia which led off with the movement. There, in 1790, a group of influential citizens, including an Episcopalian, a Universalist, two Quakers, and a Roman Catholic, launched "The First Day or Sunday School Society," which was formally organized in January, 1791. Its purpose, as stated in the preamble to the constitution, was to be:

Whereas, the good education of youth is of the first importance to society, and numbers of children, the offspring of indigent parents, have not proper opportunities of instruction previous to their being apprenticed to trades; and whereas, among the youth of every large city, various instances occur of the first day of the week, called Sunday,—a day which ought to be devoted to religious improvement,—being employed to the worst of purposes, the depravity of morals and manners: It is therefore the opinion of sundry persons, that the establishment of Sunday-schools in this city would be of essential advantage to the rising generation; and for effecting that benevolent purpose they have formed themselves into a society.[1]

This philanthropic purpose of doing something for others less fortunate dominated these early organizations, usually known as "Sunday School Unions." Other cities followed suit by establishing similar organizations of the Union type. The early interest of women in the movement is shown by the organization in New York in 1816 of "The Female Union Society, for the Promotion of Sabbath Schools."

The impetus to carry the Sunday school to needy people soon extended beyond the bounds of the cities. In 1817 the "Philadelphia Sunday and Adult School Union" was formed with the purpose to "cultivate unity and charity among those of different names, to ascertain the extent of gratuitous instruction in Sunday and adult schools, to promote their establishment in the city and in the villages in the country, to give more effect to Christian exertion in general, and to encourage and strengthen each other in the cause of the Redeemer." It embraced the members of several Unions in Philadelphia and other parts of Pennsylvania. In 1821 its missionary organized upward of sixty schools in six different states. It also issued Scripture "tickets" and other material.[2]

There remained one more step to be taken, that of forming a Union which would be national in scope. This was accomplished with the organization in 1824 of the American Sunday School Union, with headquarters in

---

[1]Marianna C. Brown, *Sunday School Movements in America*, p. 27. Fleming H. Revell Co., New York, 1901. Used by permission.

[2]*Idem*, p. 30.

Philadelphia. Its object was "to concentrate the efforts of Sabbath-school societies in different portions of our country . . . to disseminate useful information; circulate moral and religious publications in every part of the land, and endeavor to plant a Sunday-school wherever there is a population."[3] This organization has a magnificent history of service, continuing uninterruptedly to the present day.

2. *Conventions.*—We turn our attention next to a new type of approach to the organization and improvement of the Sunday school. This is the Sunday school convention. Whereas the Sunday School Union was an effort on the part of public spirited and religiously devout men and women to do something *for* the great untouched masses of people of all ages, the convention movement was more concerned with providing for mutual helpfulness to each other of those who were actually the workers in the Sunday schools. The line between the two is not a sharp one. It seems that the first conventions were sponsored by the Unions.

In 1832 a national convention was called, to meet in New York. Well over two hundred delegates responded to the call, representing fifteen states, which was more than half the number then in the Union. The topics on the program sound strangely modern, and it may be that we are deluding ourselves when we think that we would today be much better able to answer such problems. So pleased were the delegates with the inspiration, fellowship, and practical help received in this convention that they voted not to disband at its close but to adjourn to meet again in Philadelphia the following spring.

[3]Marianna C. Brown, *op. cit.*, p. 32.

This adjourned meeting, held as scheduled six months later, was not so successful either in attendance or interest. Due to discouragement on account of this comparative failure or for some other reason, which history does not seem to reveal, twenty years elapsed before another attempt was made to hold a national convention. One recommendation approved by this second convention would delight the hearts of those who are in our day concerned with "reaching the unreached": "that a systematic and simultaneous canvass of the entire country be made, to obtain scholars and enlist parents in the work, on the 4th of July following."[4]

Next in line of development were the county and state Sunday school conventions. The first county convention of which we have record was held in Winchester, Scott County, Illinois, in 1846. A number of state conventions were held in the 1850's, in some cases starting a succession of annual conventions which has been unbroken. These county and state conventions were to spread throughout the country until there was scarcely a place left which they did not reach.

National conventions were resumed, with the third one held in Philadelphia in 1859, and a fourth ten years later in Newark. Thereafter these conventions were held every third year, until 1914, and since that time every four years until interrupted by World War II. However, as we shall see, the convention plays a smaller role in interdenominational work under the present organization than it did before 1922. It was the convention of 1872, in Indianapolis, which adopted the plan for International Uniform Lessons. In 1875, in Baltimore, there were twenty Canadian delegates present, and from that

---

[4]Marianna C. Brown, *op. cit.*, p. 55.

time these coventions have been international in character as well as in name, to include the United States and Canada.

It is hard to overestimate the service of these conventions—county, state, national, and international—in developing enthusiasm for the Sunday school, a spirit of fellowship among the workers, and spreading newer methods and materials. Probably the enthusiastic editorial in the *Sunday School Times,* in comment on the convention in 1869, might in fairness be applied to many of them, with variation only in the numbers attending and the area served:

> Never before had so many Sunday-school leaders of the land been brought face to face. Taken as a whole, it was the most memorable Sunday-school gathering ever assembled in the United States, if not in the world. Tongues of fire seemed to be given to the speakers. The spirit of brotherly love and union prevailed. It was estimated that there were over twenty-five hundred visitors, in addition to the five hundred twenty-six delegates, in attendance.[5]

3. *The associations.*—An outgrowth of the Sunday school convention was the Sunday School Association, a permanent organization of Sunday school workers. At first the interim organizations seem to have been very simple, with a primary purpose of calling and arranging for the next convention. Gradually they became more elaborate, with an employed secretary and staff, and a year-round program. The authorizing body and chief means of support was the convention, and there was no official relation to denominational bodies. The place of the local church in these associations is not so clear.

[5] Arlo A. Brown, *A History of Religious Education in Recent Times,* pp. 168f. Abingdon Press. New York, 1923. Used by permission.

They were called upon to send delegates and to make contributions, but the association itself seems generally to have been one of individuals and not of churches.

These associations existed on the township, county, state and provincial, and national or international (United States and Canada), and world (World's Sunday School Association) levels. Each stood in the relation of auxiliary to the next larger geographical body, but each was autonomous and completely sovereign in its own area. They drew into their leadership some of the most able laymen and ministers. In the work of the Illinois state organization, for example, we find such noted men as B. F. Jacobs, William Reynolds, and Dwight L. Moody. These associations had a capacity for mobilizing the interest and effort of laymen which the more ecclesiastically controlled organizations of our day find it difficult to equal.

The International Sunday School Conventions led to the formation of the International Sunday School Association. Its first official full-time employed field representative, William Reynolds, was chosen in 1887, and its first general secretary, Marion Lawrance, in 1899, in the Atlanta convention. This was rapidly followed by the election of a staff of paid workers and incorporation by an act of Congress in 1907. This charter states: "That the purpose of the Association shall be to promote organized Sunday school work, to encourage the study of the Bible, and to assist in the spread of Christian religion."

The more intensive cultivation of the field which was made possible by the development of the International Sunday School Association and its auxiliary state and county associations made it inevitable that there should be duplication and eventual clash with the developing programs of the denominations. This led to its reorganization in 1922 so as to make it more representative of all the forces of Christian education. Along with its new form, the organization also took a new name—the International Council of Religious Education.

The movements which we have thus far reviewed have been designated as nondenominational. This is correct in the sense that they were not officially representative of the churches or the denominations. They were not, however, outside the churches. The leading spirits in them were the outstanding laymen and ministers of the day, and the people they served were first of all workers in their own churches. It has been said also that these were laymen's movements. This is true only in so far as laymen and clergy were equally free to participate. In proportion to their numbers in the churches, the clergy were probably even better represented than the laity.

II. Denominational Agencies

The agencies within the denominations which are responsible for the promotion and supervision of Christian education are the boards of Sunday schools, young people's work, and, more recently, the inclusive boards of Christian education. In most cases, it is difficult to fix the exact date of origin of these boards as promotional and supervisory agencies for Christian education, because they were usually the outgrowth of activity of a different or more limited nature. Churches were interested in Christian education before the establishment of the Sunday school. So far as the Sunday school is concerned, many of them no doubt thought of the nondenominational Unions and Conventions as representing their interest and deserving their effort.

John Wesley almost immediately approved the Sunday school and put himself vigorously behind it. The following interesting item appears in the minutes of the Methodist Conference in Charleston, South Carolina, of 1790:

> Let us labor, as the heart and soul of one man, to establish Sunday schools, in or near the place of public worship. Let persons be appointed by the bishops, elders, deacons, or preachers to teach (*gratis*) all that will attend and have capacity to learn, from six o'clock in the morning till ten; and from two o'clock in the afternoon till six, where it does not interfere with public worship.
>
> The council shall compile a proper schoolbook to teach them learning and piety.[6]

As early as 1844, the bishops of the Methodist Episcopal Church, in their address to the General Conference, included the following statement, which will be recognized at once as a very advanced position for the improvement of Sunday school work:

> Sunday-school instruction may justly be regarded as one of the most effectual auxiliaries which we can employ for the prevention of the destructive influence of error, by preoccupying the infant mind with the germs of scriptural truth. Although it is a matter of rejoicing that a great amount of good has been accomplished by this service, it is believed that much more might be done with a system better adapted to the capacities of the subjects of instruction, and with books suitable to different classes in the several stages of improvement. Classification for many reasons has always been regarded as an important pro-

---

[6]A. A. Brown, *A History of Religious Education in Recent Times*, p. 49. Abingdon Press, New York, 1923. Used by permission.

vision in a system of instruction, especially for children. We need not enlarge on its utility, but we are deeply impressed with the necessity and obligation of renewed and persevering effort in extending the operation of the institution so as to embrace tens of thousands of the children of our people who have not been brought under its salutary influence, and of revising and improving the system both with respect to the mode of instruction and the books to be used, so as to afford the best helps and the greatest facility in accomplishing its benevolent designs.[7]

While these instances have been taken from Methodist history, other denominations also were not failing to see the value of the Sunday school and were giving it their vigorous support. By 1850 the organization of denominational boards for the promotion and supervision of Christian education was well under way, and by the beginning of the twentieth century, there was scarcely a denomination which did not make such provision. The work of many of these boards had grown to large proportions and was ever increasing. The services they rendered can be roughly divided into two groups:

1. *Editorial and publishing.*—While many independent publishers have sought to supply the needs for church school materials, it has been generally recognized that this is primarily a function of the denomination. This group of services includes the planning for the kind of materials to be provided, which is done in curriculum committees; the writing and editing of these materials; and finally, the publication and distribution of them to the churches. Through the rendering of these services under its own control, a denomination may assure its churches that they will receive materials properly

[7] A. A. Brown, *op. cit.*, pp. 94f.

adapted to their needs and interpretations of the Scripture and doctrine which are in harmony with the points of view of the denomination concerned. Even in the case of the International Uniform Lessons, while outlines have been prepared by an interdenominational committee, the writing of lessons and the printing and publication have always been the prerogative of the denominational boards. In the field of teacher training, much of the text material has been cooperatively prepared and frequently used in interdenominational groups; but each denomination reserves the right to give its own approval to such common materials before they are recommended to its churches, or to prepare its own training materials in areas where common materials are not available or are unsatisfactory.

2. *Promotion and supervision.*—This service requires a field program and a field staff. It involves also the preparation of standards and emphases, which express the interests and needs of the churches of a particular denomination, and may differ widely from those promoted by other denominations. It is in this area that overlapping with the work of nondenominational agencies is most pronounced, and where conflict is most likely to develop. It is granted that this type of service readily yields to a large amount of joint planning and promotion by the representatives of the several denominations, but this does not come to pass through having a nondenominational agency make such plans *for* the churches but rather through interdenominational cooperation in the development of a common program.

With the great increase in interest and activity in Christian education during the first part of the twentieth century, the consciousness of denominational boards of their responsibility for their own churches, as over against having those churches served by nondenominational agencies, grew more pronounced. This growing sense of denominational responsibility for its own church schools and the need for cooperative relationship with each other led the secretaries, editors, and publishers of these church school boards of the denominations to form, in 1910, an association of their own, called the Sunday School Council of Evangelical Denominations, with an initial membership of about 150. The cardinal principles underlying the organization of this agency were (1) denominational autonomy in matters of Sunday school administration and instruction and (2) direct cooperative denominational control of interdenominational Sunday school activities. This is expressed in the following words in the preamble to the constitution:

> Recognizing the responsibility of each denomination, through its properly constituted Sunday-school authorities, to direct its own Sunday-school work, and believing that much Sunday-school effort is common work, therefore, for the sake of economy, educational betterment, and Christian brotherhood, we organize ourselves into a body under the following constitution.[8]

The objectives of the organization were stated in general to be that of the advancement of the Sunday school interests of the denominations cooperating, and specifically (1) by conferring together in matters of common interest; (2) by giving expression to common views and decisions; (3) by cooperative action in matters concern-

---

[8]*The Encyclopedia of Sunday Schools and Religious Education*, article on "Sunday School Council of Evangelical Denominations." Thomas Nelson & Sons, New York, 1915. Used by permission.

ing educational, editorial, missionary, and publishing activities.

A logical sequence to the purpose for which the new council was organized would have been the development of a field program and the employment of a field staff to coordinate the existing denominational programs. This, however, would have brought it directly into the field of work of the International Sunday School Association, thus making two interdenominational approaches. This developing situation led to a number of years of conflict and debate. Some of the members of the new Council were, of course, also ardent supporters of the Association. Farseeing men recognized that there must be a better way to resolve this conflict than by open battle for the control of Sunday school work in the churches. The chapter recording the resulting efforts to preserve Christian unity and brotherhood in the best interests of the cause which all held dear, while it may have its stains at many points, constitutes one of the brightest in American church history. The process leading to merger is well described in the words of Arlo Brown, who speaks from the vantage point of a participant:

In 1918 it was evident that either the Sunday-School Council, hitherto an advisory body only, must enlarge its scope and build up an organization to do executive work or else the International Sunday-School Association must reorganize itself so as to be officially the representative of the denominations. For several years these two bodies had maintained a Joint Committee on Standards. Each had also maintained a Committee on Reference and Counsel which had held numerous conferences together. Through these and other means, both organizations had begun to understand each other more perfectly. In 1918 each body named its own Committee on Reference and Counsel to represent it on a joint committee to bring about a reorganization of both agencies with the view of uniting upon a common program.

In 1920 a plan for reorganization was effected in the annual meetings of the executive bodies of each organization. This plan provided that fifty per cent of the members of the Executive Committee of the International Sunday-School Association should be territorial representatives, selected as formerly to represent the International Sunday-School Convention and the territorial, State, and Provincial Associations, while fifty per cent should be selected as official representatives of the cooperating denominations. It was also provided that the full-time paid workers of the International Sunday-School Association and its auxiliaries should be admitted to the membership of the Sunday-School Council of Evangelical Denominations.

However, it is one thing to perfect an organization upon paper and quite a different thing to carry it out. In June, 1920, both the Executive Committee of the International Sunday-School Association and the Sunday-School Council met on the same days and in the same place, Buffalo, New York, to welcome the new members in each group. In January and February, 1921, the reorganized Council and the reorganized Executive Committee of the International held their annual meetings. It was decided here that two steps were necessary to move toward the complete union of the two bodies; first that the auxiliary associations in the States must be helped to reorganize and then to develop a program in common with the denominations, and, second, that one common Committee on Education should be created. This committee was duly constituted, assigned supervision over all educational matters, and asked to report for approval to the two bodies creating them.[9]

In 1922 the union of the two bodies was consummated in a new organization known as the International Sunday

[9]A. A. Brown, *A History of Religious Education in Recent Times*, pp. 186f. Abingdon Press, New York, 1923. Used by permission.

School Council of Religious Education. Shortly thereafter the words "Sunday School" were dropped from the name, both for the sake of brevity and to take account of the expanding program of Christian education beyond the Sunday school. The intervening years have allowed time for the provisions of this merger to be carried into actual effect and to extend it into the state and local auxiliaries. These years have also shown the wisdom of the steps which were taken, for a great new impetus has been given to Christian education, and it has been discovered that cooperative activity without sacrificing denominational responsibility is possible over wide areas of Christian education work.

The preamble to the bylaws of the new organization states the basis on which the merger was consummated and how the conflicts out of which it came were resolved:

1. We recognize it to be the right and duty of each denomination through its properly constituted Sunday school authorities to direct its Sunday school work.

2. We recognize that in the field of religious education, there is need for cooperative efforts between the various denominations, between the several denominations and organizations, and among the general organizations themselves and that there are problems in religious education that can best be solved by such cooperative effort.

3. We recognize that in the field of religious education, the local community, and local institutions and organizations have rights of initiative and local self-government.

4. We recognize the rights of the cooperating local churches and organizations to be represented as such in the direction and control of any community movement, which has for its purpose the training of workers for the local churches or the religious instruction of the children of the churches.

5. The International Sunday School Association henceforth and until the Charter is amended shall operate under the name and title "The International Council of Religious Education."

Let it be clear, however, that the formation of the International Council of Religious Education did not provide a single organization for the promotion and improvement of church school work. The boards of Christian education of the denominations continue as before to carry on an aggressive program on a denominational basis. It is they who are the source of 50 per cent of the constituent membership of the new council. What has been accomplished is to make provision for activities in Christian education which cut across denominational lines to be truly interdenominational in character rather than nondenominational. The new organization vests control in the duly elected representatives of the denominations and of the auxiliary state councils. Consequently, the International Convention, which at one time was the authoritative body, has lost that character but continues to be an occasion for inspiration, fellowship, and education. It is one of the activities of the International Council of Religious Education, but has no control over the organization or activities of the Council except as it becomes an expression of public opinion.

III. THE PRESENT SITUATION

A quarter century has passed since the organization of the International Council of Religious Education, giving the forces of Protestant Christian education a cooperative agency which could truly and officially represent them in work which can best be done by working together. Only gradually has the new agency become in the minds of the leaders of these forces their very own instrument through which they work together, rather than an outside organization with which they cooperate. The balance between services rendered to the local churches by their denominational boards and by cooperative community agencies remains in unstable equilibrium, as experience demonstrates what the proper fields of each may be. Since Protestant Christians are grouped by denominations, it is necessary that there be a denominational program. Since churches are also in a community setting, and since the denominations face many situations which can be handled only by joint action, it is equally necessary that there be an interdenominational cooperative program. At the present time the picture is somewhat as follows:

1. On the one hand, we have the denominational activities carried on through the denominational boards or commissions of Christian education. These agencies are not uniform in structure, policies, or procedure but, generally speaking, they exist for common purposes. They counsel their churches as to ways of effectively carrying on their work in Christian education through Sunday schools, vacation schools, youth societies, and other avenues and media. They sponsor curriculum committees which study the needs of persons and the objectives of their denominations in order that they may translate these needs and objectives into curriculum specifications. They prepare general program helps for pastors, superintendents, and church school teachers. They conduct schools, classes, institutes, and conferences for the training of leaders. They maintain field staffs which spend their time in direct service to the churches of their denominations.

Paralleling the educational agencies of the denominations are editorial and publishing house staffs which prepare and merchandise periodical literature, teachers' helps, and books necessary to the educational program of the local church. Here also the scope of work and degree of specialization vary with the size of the denomination. Their educational services are usually carried on under the guidance of the denominational curriculum committee.

The educational and editorial staffs of these denominational agencies vary in size from the largest, which numbers 123 persons, to the smallest, where one man acts as both general secretary and editor for his church. The larger denominations work through numerous departments with one or more staff members in each. However, the type of staff organization most frequently found is that in which there are but a few workers, each dividing his time among two or three responsibilities.

2. On the other hand, we have the interdenominational program, carried out through the International Council of Religious Education and its auxiliary state and provincial councils and the city and county councils. Since 1922 the implications of the merger have been gradually carried into effect in these agencies. It has taken time to adjust the more extreme viewpoints on both sides of the controversy which led to the new organization. There have been those who have felt that the Council was moving too far away from the underlying principles of the Sunday School Association, in the direction of ecclesiastical control. There have been those also who have felt that the Council has been too much dominated by its Association history and has been inadequately ex-

pressive of the common mind and work of the constituent denominations. However, at no time has this difference of opinion between those representing denominations and those representing territories resulted in a vote on any issue which was divided on the fifty-fifty basis of the membership provided by the plan of the merger. Through the years it has become increasingly evident that this continental body, paralleling the denominations in the scope of its work, must be primarily the cooperative agency of these denominations. The principle of territorial representation is recognized to be sound but not to the extent of providing an effective balance to denominational interests and pressures. It is increasingly evident that the territorial unit can in turn find its own best expression through becoming an auxiliary to the International Council and the cooperative agency of the state or district and other local units of the denominations.

The support which has been given the International Council by the denominational boards of Christian education through the work of their executives and staff members and through financial contributions is nothing short of magnificent, and the extent to which in its twenty-five years of history this organization has become the cooperative agency of these denominations is very promising for the future of interchurch work.

From modest beginnings the work of the Council has grown until it now includes twenty departments under the direction of a staff of twenty-six persons. The influence of the Council is felt as never before in the public press, in government circles, in public education, as well as in the fields of the churches' life and work. The loyalty of the regional organizations, state, city, and provincial councils, has been gratifying.

In turn the International Council furnishes staff leadership to scores of state and city activities during the course of a single year. Relations with other interchurch agencies have been close, many activities have been jointly sponsored, and in some instances a staff member of one agency has served another over an extended period in a joint relationship.

As a part of the study of Christian education on which this book is based, a committee consisting primarily of denominational and council executives made a thoroughgoing inquiry into the purpose and work of the International Council. It is their recommendation, approved by the Committee on the Study of Christian Education, that the first article of the bylaws be restated as follows:

Purpose and Functions: In pursuance of its purpose as stated in its charter, it shall be the function of the International Council of Religious Education to serve as the agency of the churches of North America through which their leaders in Christian education may (*a*) enjoy the inspiration and self-education which comes through fellowship, (*b*) share convictions, ideas, and experiences, (*c*) evaluate their current plans and practices, (*d*) examine areas of needed service, (*e*) carry on cooperative research, (*f*) carry on activities for enrichment of their denominational programs, (*g*) plan together religious education activities of a community nature, (*h*) cooperate in developing a public mind favorable to the conduct of Christian education, (*i*) unite in carrying on certain designated aspects of their work, (*j*) conduct experimentation in needed new fields vital to Christian education, (*k*) provide a means whereby two or more denominations may join in common endeavors of their choice, and (*l*) join in such other plans and activities as may seem wise and helpful.

As a further definition of the functions of the International Council, this committee prepared the following statement for use by the officers, general secretary, and staff members of the Council:

1. To provide its member Christian education agencies with the inspiration, spiritual enrichment, and self-education which comes through fellowship.

2. To encourage and promote those values which come to the Christian education movement through cooperative activity.

3. To provide an avenue through which staffs of member agencies may exchange ideas and experiences, evaluate their plans and practices, and improve the quality of their educational programs for the churches and individuals whom they serve.

4. To serve as a medium through which the staffs of member agencies may formulate plans for providing adequate Christian education for those now related to the churches and for those thus far unreached, as well as to serve as a medium through which they may determine which phases of such plans may be undertaken cooperatively or unitedly.

5. To help inform persons, both within and outside the churches, regarding the past achievements, present activities, and future possibilities of the Christian education movement in North America and thus to help create a general climate favorable to Christian education.

6. To help inspire men and women, particularly parents, to a larger measure of responsibility for the work of Christian education; to enlist both lay and professional forces in efforts for extension of Christian education services to those not now reached and for increasing the effectiveness of their work with those already within the fold of the church.

7. To provide a means whereby all member agencies or any group of member agencies may unite in administering such tasks as they may wish to carry on unitedly.

8. To conduct or arrange for the conduct of such research as is essential to the intelligent pursuance of its other functions.

9. To plan together religious education programs of a community nature and to administer such continent-wide activities as are essential to the success of such programs.

10. To maintain relationships on behalf of the Christian education movement with other religious forces, with character-building agencies, and with the government.

In order to strengthen the International Council of Religious Education in discharging these responsibilities the Committee on the Study of Christian Education made numerous recommendations for the modification of its existing structure for the consideration of the Council. A larger place for laymen was recommended, along with a larger use of theologians, biblical scholars, and other specialists. The relationships of territorial councils received some recommendations. Certain changes were suggested in the committees, sections, and boards of the Council. Modifications of its program of annual meetings were advanced.

That the International Council is in no sense a superorganization which can dictate to its constituent member agencies, but must lead solely through the appeal of its program and activities on their merits, is made clear in the following statements of policy with respect to certain issues, which was formulated by this same committee:

1. With respect to the participation of member agencies, it is recognized that "the success of the Council as an interdenominational enterprise depends upon the extent to which member agencies participate in its committees and other working groups and make use of

its educational products. Therefore, it is the earnest desire of the Council that the constituent denominations shall cooperate in all its activities and that there shall be widespread use by member agencies of the recommendations and materials which have been cooperatively planned and prepared. The Council recognizes, however, the right of member agencies to determine the extent and the points of their participation in its committees and other working groups and the use they will make of its educational products.''

2. Concerning statements of Christian faith and educational philosophy, the following recommendation was made:

> The Council will prepare from time to time statements of the Christian faith and of educational philosophy as bases for its own program building or field activities and as possible guides for the developing program of Christian education in the churches. While such statements, in the preparation of which member agencies have participated, may properly be recommended by the Council to the constituent agencies for their consideration and possible adoption in the development of their own programs of Christian education, it is recognized that these statements will not be set forth as representing the faith or convictions of individual member agencies except as they may have taken official action thereon.

3. With regard to public pronouncements, it is recognized that the Council is by nature an educational agency and that such public pronouncements should be limited to those issues which affect the functioning of the churches as educational agencies. Pronouncements of the Council shall be recognized as statements of that body, and not of its member agencies. As such, pro-

nouncements of the Council need not have the endorsement of its individual member agencies, nor does the Council in such statements represent officially its constituent denominations except as they individually endorse specific actions and authorize the Council so to represent them. In case the members are divided on pronouncements which are to be made, the Council shall make clear the extent of both majority and minority opinion.

4. Concerning field emphases and services, the Council may formulate and produce united national emphases when desired by its member agencies, determine the pattern of promotion of such emphases, and facilitate its members in uniting in field promotion of such emphases for the purpose of making a united impression on American Protestantism.

These statements of functions and policies indicate the general fields in which the International Council of Religious Education is operating or is seeking to operate. It represents forty-two denominations in the United States and Canada, including over 90 per cent of the Protestant church membership of the continent. In Canada its work is supplemented by the Religious Education Council of Canada, which deals with problems and tasks which must be carried forward in the light of their own indigenous needs and circumstances. The International Council is not to be confused with the World's Sunday School Association. The former is "international" only in the sense that it includes the United States and Canada, while the latter renders a similar service for the world-wide field. The International Council is one of the constituent territorial units of the World's Sunday School Association.

In summary, it may be said that the International Council is for the denominations their medium for interdenominational fellowship, for the sharing of experience, for research and study, for cooperative planning, for maintenance of relationships with extrachurch agencies, and for the administration of those educational tasks which they wish to have conducted on their behalf.

Auxiliary to the International Council, and coordinating the efforts of the denominations in their territory in a similar manner, are the interdenominational agencies of several geographical categories—state or provincial, city, county. Originally these agencies were Sunday school associations organized on a lay membership basis. Following the formation of the International Council of Religious Education in 1922, most of these agencies became councils of religious education and attempted so to reorganize their structures and program as to make themselves "the denominations in cooperation" on their respective geographic levels. During the past fifteen years, most of these council agencies have merged their work into councils of churches, in which religious education is carried as a part of a more inclusive program.

State Sunday school associations originally attempted to service local church schools on their total needs, except the supplying of curriculum material. As they become councils of religious education or councils of churches they have tended more and more to become media for the promotion and guidance of community cooperation. In such cases, they have stressed the stimulation of public interest, promotion of special emphases, community surveys, community training schools, weekday schools of religion, work among the underprivileged, and, more recently, services for wartime industrial areas.

Thirty-one state organizations are officially recognized by the majority of the denominations in their areas as their agencies for cooperative work. All of these agencies have employed staff leadership. Seventy-two related city organizations also have employed staffs.

State and city councils vary greatly in size. The largest provision for religious education within any state organization is through one of the few remaining councils of religious education which has a departmentalized program under a staff of eight persons. The largest provision within a city organization is through a division of Christian education of a church council which has a staff of several persons. On the other hand, there are several states and cities where the total program, including religious education services, is carried on under the leadership of a single executive.

Associated with the state councils are approximately sixteen hundred county councils of churches or religious education without paid executive leadership. In some cases these are voluntary associations of churches. In most cases they are associations of ministers and laymen as individuals.

As we have seen, on the city and state level, the council of religious education has gradually given way to an inclusive council of churches, in which Christian education is included as a department of work. This trend, and the emphasis on a unified church program, has raised the question of whether a similar step should not be taken on the national and continental level. The International Council shares this field with a number of other agencies, including the Federal Council of the Churches of Christ in America, the Home Missions Council, the Foreign Missions Conference, the Missionary Education

Movement, the Council of Church Boards of Education, the United Council of Church Women, the United Stewardship Council, each with its own group of co-operating denominations, and each with its program implications in the local churches and communities. There is increasing conviction that united strength and economy of effort could be achieved if these agencies could merge their work in one inclusive Protestant effort.

Progress in the direction of such united agencies has been made during the past several years. Planning has been going forward looking to the organization of this new body under the name of the National Council of the Churches of Christ in the United States of America. The International Council has been a party to these negotiations and has voted to submit the plan for ratification to its member agencies. It is proposed that its work be continued in the Division of Christian Education of the new organization. Provision would be made in the new Division for the participation of member denominations who are now members of the International Council but who may not wish to become members in full of the over-all organization.

IV. WHAT OF THE FUTURE?

Christian education by its nature has a tendency to draw people into cooperative effort. Always there have been those who have envisioned a single Protestant program of nation-wide proportions, paralleling our great system of public education. The fellowship which has resulted from cooperative effort has been genuine and fruitful. While the purpose of the united efforts for Christian education has not been church union, these efforts have probably contributed as much as any other influence to the spirit of unity which now exists among the churches.

It remains a fact, however, that the Protestant forces of the continent are divided into denominational groups. If there are good reasons for maintaining these denominational groups, then it follows inevitably that each must have its own program of education and promotion. Hence there will be many parallel programs of Christian education.

On the other hand, the need for a united approach on any level, but particularly on the community level, must constantly draw these forces together into cooperation. This has led to the repeated efforts for a united program, culminating in the council of Christian education or the Christian education department of a council of churches, which is officially representative of the denominational boards of Christian education, and at the same time provides a united community approach.

There has been an attempt at a broad division of function as between service to the local church and service to the churches working unitedly in common enterprises. The first is regarded as the peculiar prerogative of the denomination, the latter of the churches working together. This division cannot successfully be maintained, because there are so many services which can properly be given to local churches through joint effort of those churches or through a cooperative agency representing all the boards with which these churches are affiliated.

A great gain was made when the cooperative program became officially representative of the churches, through the council plan. If it resulted in a temporary withdrawal of some cooperative services to the local church, those services will be restored and increased as the denominations through their cooperative agencies find more and more areas in which they can develop a common program. The extent of this must increase with experience in working together, resulting in better understanding of each other's programs and in more common production of literature, standards, and field emphases. In some fields this increasing cooperative endeavor is already effectively and practically expressed by having the same employed worker serving both as the field director for his denomination for that area and as a member of the staff of the council for the same area. At least one denomination has made a similar arrangement with the International Council of Religious Education by lending one of its staff members to serve also on the staff of the International Council, on a permanent basis, while other denominations have made similar temporary loans of staff members.

We have already seen that the improvement of the curriculum in the local church might be greatly enhanced by further development of cooperative effort in the production and publication of literature. Plans now in process indicate the promise of a bright future for this. However, the area of greatest need for cooperative endeavor is that of field service to the churches. A great host of professional and expert workers are traveling about the country, often going miles to serve a single church, when they might as well serve all the churches of the community which they visit. Such extension of cooperative effort is of particular significance for the smaller denominations, which are unable to maintain staff members in all parts of the country, while frequently their churches are scattered throughout the states. The principles of cooperative endeavor have now been so well formulated that there is little danger that any denomination will suffer in its program if its interests are pooled with those of other denominations in joint promotion and supervision. The needs of the day, and of the predictable future, require that far more extensive and effective interdenominational cooperation be devised and put into practice. This can be said without reflection on those who have been in the forefront of the great progress that has already been made in this direction, and in the confident hope that what is now an imperative need will become an accomplished fact in the not too distant future.

Chapter IX

Christian Education—Today and Tomorrow

IN THE preceding chapters we have viewed the movement of Christian education which has been developing in the Protestant churches of America during the past 150 years, but with particular reference to its more recent history. We have been critical in our review. We have asked whether Christian education as now practiced is adequate to meet the needs for which it has been called into being. We have tried to see those needs in the light of the situation as it exists today, in the churches, in the community, in the world at large, and in the progress of theological and educational thought.

No one can view the march of this movement across the years without a feeling of profound respect and appreciation for those who have carried it on. Any movement which draws the loyalty and participation of over twenty million people, the labors of more than two million men and women who give their services voluntarily, and can supersede its traditions by evolving constantly new forms of expressions for the achievement of its objectives is one that has life and vigor.

Nevertheless, when viewed against the background of the imperative need for Christian education in America today, the movement of Christian education is found wanting in both its efforts and achievements. This widespread sense of inadequacy is in part due to the fact that idealistic leaders always have a vision which exceeds their reach. But it is more than that. There is a growing conviction that in present-day Christian education we have a fifty horsepower machine to do a work which requires many hundreds of horsepower.

Any evaluation will, of course, draw many degrees of opinion, ranging all the way from those who feel that "all's right with the world" to those who feel that the whole matter is worthless and that a new start must be made. There is, however, one point of agreement. That is the crucial need for an effective work in Christian education.

In the evaluation here presented we have sought to be realistic, but not unto discouragement or despair. It is our conviction that the movement for Christian education is young enough to grow. If mistakes have been made in the past, it is flexible enough to correct its own mistakes once they have been fully uncovered. If new occasions require new duties, if new discoveries in educational science require new methods, if new insights in theology require a rethinking of purposes and content, the leaders of Christian education can in due humility respond with proper sensitivity to these trends.

What are the hopeful directions in which Christian education in the period ahead should move? So far as the findings of the Committee on the Study of Christian Education are concerned, these have been embodied in the previous chapters and will be more fully stated in the published reports. Perhaps it is gratuitous to add a concluding chapter embodying such recommendations. In any case the editor must take full responsibility for these statements because the committee which he represents did not make such a formulation. In so far only as they repeat material covered in previous chapters can they be regarded as a product of the committee.

1. *Christian education in, for, and by the church.*—In theory, the ideal of "a church and only a church" has been held for a number of years; but, in practice, it has not yet come to reality in many local churches. It is our conviction that this trend is profoundly significant for the future of Christian education. It will counteract the tendency to set Christian education off as the unfaithful adopted child who can be made a whipping boy for all that is wrong and bring it back as a legitimate responsibility of the whole church. There needs to be a profound change in point of view as well as in sense of responsibility before this ideal will truly find expression in any local church. But beginnings toward it can be made anywhere, and many churches have already made them in practice.

One of the most significant elements in this interpretation of the place of Christian education in the church is its new recognition of the place of the minister in this program. Many ministers welcome this new opportunity and are in fact already engaged in carrying out its responsibility. Others will need a profound conversion to a new point of view, and this conversion best begins in the seminary where the ministers are trained. But congregations also need to be converted to a new point of view, for few of them have placed interest and competence in Christian education high in the category of qualifications on the basis of which ministers are called and judged.

Perhaps the most significant change which must be worked by this new point of view is with respect to the place of the minister or director of Christian education in the local church. We have accepted the place of lay men and women in the educational program. It is abundantly clear, however, that such lay service needs to be supplemented and guided by those who are expert in Christian education. While this must first of all be the responsibility of the minister, in any church of considerable proportions the minister is unable to do all the duties which fall upon him. He needs assistance, and it is but natural that such an assistant should be assigned to the fairly specialized field of Christian education. In providing the churches with such workers, denominations and councils have done an extremely inadequate work of recruitment, the colleges and seminaries have done an inadequate job of training, and local churches have done far less than they should in providing status, security, and favorable conditions of work. Unless this problem can be promptly attacked and properly solved, the whole cause of Christian education will lag behind the opportunities which are now open to it.

2. *Lay workers.*—As we have seen, the tradition of having the lay members of the church teach and give other leadership in Christian education has carried over from the earlier days of the Sunday school and now extends even to other aspects of the church's educational work. If this tradition is to be maintained, and it probably will, then a renewed effort must be made to prepare workers who are competent for the present-day program. This will involve three lines of approach. First, the effort to train lay workers for the various aspects of Christian education must be continued, intensified, and made more practical. The importance of Christian teaching needs to be enhanced so that lay workers will not too readily assume that any effort on their part is good enough. We have seen that under the proper motivation lay people will give large amounts of time and energy

to prepare themselves for specific service in the community. The same must apply to their service in the churches.

Second, the tasks in Christian education which are to be undertaken by lay persons must in many cases be redefined so as to assume the aspects which a layman can understand and perform. In most churches there are some persons who will become semiprofessional as teachers through their ready grasp of educational implications, extraordinary work in training themselves, and native qualities which enable them to adapt readily to the requirements of the practice of teaching as now conceived. On the other hand, there will be many others who will be discouraged if the standards of professional training are set too high. Can a place be found for them in which they can make a genuine contribution through the exercise of such interests and abilities as they have? We believe that this can be done. It will be through specific instruction and supervision in a particular type of work which they are to do, such as leading worship, conducting discussions, carrying on handwork or other activities. It is clear that growth in Christian living may come through many avenues other than formal teaching, and it may be that a search for particular things which people of the church can do may enable the leaders to apply those particular things to the advantage of their program of Christian education.

Third, through all the avenues available to the church, its work in Christian education must be made so important to the whole church that the ablest members of the church can be drawn into its Christian education activities.

297

3. *The home.*—A whole chapter has been devoted to the strategic place of the home in the total program of Christian education. Little more needs to be added here except to say that we feel the trend has been properly set in this direction. It remains for leaders in denominations and councils as well as in local churches to find the way in which a workable program may be built which does succeed in putting the home in its proper place in the whole scheme of things. If nothing more were done in the next ten years than to follow out the implications of this new emphasis, with experimentation and practice in making the emphasis a reality, it might yet give us a decade of great advancement in Christian education.

4. *Christian theology.*—Little is to be gained by arguing or counterarguing the question of whether Christian education has been adequately founded in theology. By the theory which we have accepted, whatever is of central interest to the church is also of interest to Christian education. If the church lives by faith, it seems reasonable to expect that its work in Christian education should be permeated with that faith. Certain considerations are necessary if this proposition is to be taken seriously.

a) Christian faith must be more than the pronouncement of words from the pulpit or in church membership classes. It must become a vital experience on the part of all the people in the church, and particularly those who are the teachers. Moreover, it must go beyond experience to the ability to make an articulate statement of the faith.

b) It follows that this faith is not simply a thing to be grasped when maturity has been reached, but it applies, even though in a limited way, to persons of all ages. Little has yet been done to determine what the capacities are for religious experience at the different age levels, or what the possibilities are of making this experience articulate in words. Until the leaders in education and theology provide more effective help for the teachers of children and young people at these points, it is futile to blame these teachers for being inadequate in this important work.

c) Lesson materials will need to be built far more effectively in the light of the basic Christian positions of the churches, if from them there is to come a vital Christian experience on the part of the learners. This is not to say that the mere embodiment of theological convictions in church school literature will accomplish the whole job. It is merely to say that there needs to be some such foundation in the literature which is used if it is to come to expression in the experience of those for whom the literature furnishes the chief curriculum content.

d) The program of leadership education needs to make more provision for the understanding of the content of the Christian religion on the part of teachers, while at the same time not relinquishing its efforts on the methods by which religious growth may best be fostered.

5. *Educational methods.*—In spite of the criticism that modern Christian education has turned too far in the direction of methodology, the educational methods generally in vogue in our church schools are woefully inadequate. This is due in part to the fact that so few of the workers have actually been exposed to an adequate interpretation of the meaning of method and in part to the fact that an attempt has been made to teach method without its necessary relationship to content.

Moreover, Christian education has suffered from the efforts to transplant public school methods directly into the church school. This is a mistake for two reasons. First, because the church school situation usually differs radically from that of the public school in point of time, equipment, size of classes, regularity of attendance, and other factors. The church school is not a public school. It would seem, therefore, that the church school needs to discover or adapt methods which are suited to its own peculiar situation. Second, it seems reasonable to suppose that Christian education has a method which is peculiarly appropriate to its own purpose and work. In preceding chapters we have laid emphasis on the educative value of membership in the church fellowship. However, little has been done to define a method which is appropriate to taking full advantage of this inherent educational value. Most of our efforts at defining proper methods for the church school have centered at the point of effective ways of utilizing conduct situations or of teaching content.

6. *Supervision.*—There are many factors which make supervision imperative for the well-being of Christian education—even more so than is the case in public education. Among these factors may be named the fact that most of the teachers are lay people working on a margin of time, the large number of workers in any particular church school, the brief term of service given by most church school teachers, the varied educational and religious background of the church school workers, the limitations of the conditions under which church schools operate.

We have already referred to the need for supervisory service in the local church. This must be given by the pastor, unless the church can maintain a trained Christian education worker in addition to the pastor, or unless it is fortunate in having some lay person or persons available who can assume supervisory responsibilities. It is clear, however, that large numbers of churches will never have adequate supervision under these conditions. Those who must take the responsibility in the local church, in turn, need to be supported and guided by more expert persons, who, in the nature of the case, need to serve larger areas than the local church.

The provision of this type of supervision leads us into the field of more effective service on the part of the promotional and supervisory agencies. Most denominations maintain a staff for this purpose, and many of them have area directors who are expected to render such service on the field. Councils of churches usually make provision for a measure of local church guidance. When all is said and done, however, the number of such persons in proportion to the number of churches which need to be reached is entirely inadequate. We have already suggested that a whole new approach needs to be made on an interdenominational basis if this service is to be adequately rendered.

7. *Religion in general education.*—Our sectarian zeal has been too effective in removing a religious emphasis from public education. So bad has this situation become that we are in danger of producing a generation of people so secularized that they will have little appreciation for or interest in the churches of the communities in which they live.

The time has come for a drastic review of this whole situation on the part of both churchmen and schoolmen. It is our contention that to lay foundations in religious education is a part of the responsibility of the general schools. Unless they take this responsibility, it is questionable whether the task of Christian education which has been undertaken by the churches can ever be satisfactorily accomplished. If the public school is to remain secularized, there is ground for the suggestion which is now frequently heard that the parochial school should be resorted to by Protestantism. We believe, however, that there are such disadvantages in parochial education that some other solution must be found.

The responsibility for initiating a new consideration of the place of religion in education is one which the churches must bear. As leaders of thought in the community, the churches have a responsibility to public education in general, but in particular also to the religious content of the curriculum. Many public school workers would be heartened if they knew that the religious leaders of the community could agree on cooperating with the public school in devising ways and means by which a school might give an interpretation of religion and religious institutions which would be given for all the children of the community.

Christian education is as old as Christianity itself. Wherever there is vital religion there is an effort to teach that religion to others. The present-day emphasis on Christian education is, however, comparatively new. We believe that this movement is still in its early stages and that it is destined to grow in influence and effectiveness as the years go on, provided only that the churches and the church leaders will embrace it as a primary interest and concern.

BIBLIOGRAPHY

I. GENERAL PHILOSOPHY, PSYCHOLOGY, AND METHOD OF CHRISTIAN EDUCATION

Barclay, Wade Crawford. *The Church and a Christian Society.* Abingdon Press, New York-Cincinnati, 1939, 428 pp., $3.50.

Betts, George H., and Hawthorne, Marion O. *Method in Teaching Religion.* Abingdon Press, New York-Cincinnati, 1925, 488 pp., $2.50.

Bower, William Clayton. *Christ and Christian Education.* Abingdon-Cokesbury Press, Nashville, 1943, 128 pp., $1.00.

————. *Church and State in Education.* University of Chicago Press, Chicago, 1944, 95 pp., $1.00.

————. *The Curriculum of Religious Education.* Charles Scribner's Sons, New York, 1925, 283 pp., $2.25.

Brown, Arlo Ayres. *A History of Religious Education in Recent Times.* Abingdon Press, New York-Cincinnati, 1923, 276 pp., $1.25.

Coe, George A. *What Is Christian Education?* Charles Scribner's Sons, New York, 1929, 297 pp., $2.50.

de Blois, A. K., and Gorham, D. R. *Christian Religious Education.* Fleming H. Revell Co., New York, 1939, 380 pp., $3.00.

Elliott, Harrison S. *Can Religious Education Be Christian?* Macmillan Co., New York, 1940, 321 pp., $2.50.

Fergusson, Edmund Morris. *Historic Chapters in Christian Education in America.* Fleming H. Revell Co., New York, 1935, 102 pp., $1.50.

Groves, E. R. *Christianity and the Family.* Macmillan Co., New York, 1942, 220 pp., $2.50.

Homrighausen, E. G. *Choose Ye This Day.* Westminster Press, Philadelphia, 1943, 152 pp., $1.50.

Horne, Herman Harrell. *The Philosophy of Christian Education.* Fleming H. Revell Co., New York, 1937, 171 pp., $1.50.

Jones, Mary Alice. *The Faith of Our Children.* Abingdon-Cokesbury Press, Nashville, 1943, 175 pp., $1.50.

Lotz, P. H., and Crawford, L. W. (editors). *Studies in Religious Education.* Cokesbury Press, Nashville, 1931, 617 pp., $3.50.

Munro, Harry C. *The Pastor and Religious Education.* Abingdon Press, New York, 1930, 227 pp., $2.00.

Price, J. M. (editor). *Introduction to Religious Education.* Macmillan Co., New York, 1932, 476 pp., $2.25.

Sherrill, Lewis J. *Family and Church.* Abingdon Press, New York-Cincinnati, 1937, 266 pp., $2.00.

————. *The Rise of Christian Education.* Macmillan Co., New York, 1944, 305 pp., $2.50.

Smith, H. Shelton. *Faith and Nurture.* Charles Scribner's Sons, New York, 1941, 202 pp., $2.00.

THE CHURCH AND CHRISTIAN EDUCATION

Smith, Robert Seneca. *New Trails for the Christian Teacher.* West-minster Press, Philadelphia, 1934, 260 pp., $1.50.

Soares, Theodore Gerald. *Religious Education.* University of Chicago Press, Chicago, 1928, 336 pp., $2.50.

Wieman, Regina Westcott. *The Modern Family and the Church.* Harper and Brothers, New York, 1937, 407 pp., $2.00.

Williams, J. Paul. *The New Education and Religion.* Association Press, New York, 1945, 198 pp., $2.50.

II. ORGANIZATION AND ADMINISTRATION OF CHRISTIAN EDUCATION

Cummings, Oliver de Wolf. *Christian Education in the Local Church.* Judson Press, Philadelphia, 1942, 159 pp., $1.25; paper edition, $0.75.

Harner, Nevin C. *The Educational Work of the Church.* Abingdon Press, New York, 1939, 257 pp., $1.50.

Hewitt, Mildred. *The Church School Comes to Life.* Macmillan Co., New York, 1932, 341 pp., $2.50.

Miller, Minor C. *Teaching the Multitudes.* Beacon Publishers, Bridge-water, Va., 1944, 230 pp., $2.00.

Munro, Harry C. *Christian Education in Your Church.* Bethany Press, St. Louis, 1933, 239 pp., $1.50.

Vieth, Paul H. *Improving Your Sunday School.* Westminster Press, Philadelphia, 1930, 184 pp., $1.00.

III. RELIGIOUS EDUCATION OF YOUTH

Bowman, Clarice M. *Guiding Intermediates.* Abingdon-Cokesbury Press, Nashville, 1943, 156 pp., $0.75.

Burkhart, Roy A. *Understanding Youth.* Abingdon Press, New York, 1938, 176 pp., $1.75.

Harner, Nevin C. *Youth Work in the Church.* Abingdon-Cokesbury Press, Nashville, 1942, 222 pp. $1.75.

Harris, Erdman. *Introduction to Youth.* Macmillan Co., New York, 1940, 221 pp., $2.25.

McRae, Glenn. *Teaching Youth in the Church.* Bethany Press, St. Louis, 1940, 109 pp., $0.50.

Miller, Catherine A. *Leading Youth to Abundant Life.* Heidelberg Press, Philadelphia, 1934, 1944, 230 pp. $1.00.

Moon, Alleen. *The Christian Education of Older Youth.* Abingdon-Cokes-bury Press, Nashville, 1943, 160 pp., $0.75.

BIBLIOGRAPHY

IV. RELIGIOUS EDUCATION OF CHILDREN

Eakin, M. M. *Teaching Junior Boys and Girls.* Methodist Book Concern, New York, 1934, 277 pp., paper $0.75.

Fitch, F. M. *One God, the Ways We Worship Him.* Lothrop, Lee, & Shepard Co., New York, 1944, 137 pp., $2.00.

McCallum, Eva B. *Learning in the Nursery Class.* Bethany Press, St. Louis, 1944, 256 pp., $1.50.

Perry, Ruth D. *Children Need Adults.* Harper & Brothers, New York, 1943, 136 pp., $1.50.

Sherrill, Lewis J. *The Opening Doors of Childhood.* Macmillan Co., New York, 1939, 193 pp., $2.50.

———. *Understanding Children.* Abingdon Press, New York, 1938, 218 pp., $1.50.

Shields, Elizabeth McE. *Guiding Kindergarten Children in the Church School.* John Knox Press, Richmond, Va., 1931, 224 pp., $1.50.

———. *Music in the Religious Growth of Children.* Abingdon-Cokesbury Press, Nashville, 1943, 128 pp., $1.25.

Smither, Ethel. *Primary Children Learn at Church.* Abingdon-Cokesbury Press, Nashville, 1944, 170 pp., $1.25.

Smither, Ethel. *The Use of the Bible With Children.* Methodist Book Concern, New York, 1937, 135 pp., $1.00.

Sweet, Herman J. *Opening the Door for God.* Westminster Press, Philadelphia, 1944, 160 pp., $1.00.

V. RELIGIOUS EDUCATION OF ADULTS

Burkhart, Roy A. *The Church and the Returning Soldier.* Harper & Brothers, New York, 1945, 194 pp., $2.00.

Chamberlin, J. G. *The Church and Its Young Adults.* Abingdon-Cokesbury Press, Nashville, 1943, 124 pp., $1.00.

Hayward, P. R. and M. H. *The Home and Christian Living,* Westminster Press, Philadelphia, 1931, 158 pp., $1.00.

Powell, W. E. *Understanding Adult Ways.* Bethany Press, St. Louis, 1941, 192 pp., $2.00.

Sherrill, Lewis J., and Purcell, J. E. *Adult Education in the Church.* Presbyterian Committee of Publication, Richmond, Va., 1939, Revised Edition, 290 pp., $1.50.

Westphal, E. P. *The Church's Opportunity in Adult Education.* Westminster Press, Philadelphia, 1941, 208 pp., $1.25.

Zeigler, E. F. *Toward Understanding Adults.* Westminster Press, Philadelphia, 1931, 164 pp., $1.00.

———. *The Way of Adult Education.* Westminster Press, Philadelphia, 1938, 320 pp., $1.25.

VI. *EDUCATION FOR CHRISTIAN SERVICE*

Blair, W. D. *The New Vacation Church School.* Harper & Brothers, New York, 1934, 288 pp., $1.50.

Chave, Ernest J. *Supervision of Religious Education.* University of Chicago Press, Chicago, 1931, 352 pp., $2.50.

Dobbins, Gaines S. *The Improvement of Teaching in the Sunday School.* Broadman Press, Nashville, 1943, 170 pp., cloth, $0.60, paper, $0.40.

Knapp, Forrest L. *Leadership Education in the Church.* Abingdon Press, New York-Cincinnati, 1933, 278 pp., $1.25.

McKibben, Frank M. *Improving Religious Education Through Supervision.* Methodist Book Concern, New York, 1931, 256 pp., $1.25.

McLester, F. C. *Teaching in the Church School.* Cokesbury Press, Nashville, 1940, 160 pp., $.75.

Myers, A. J. W.: *Teaching Religion Creatively.* Fleming H. Revell Co., New York, 1932, 239 pp., $1.75.

Rogers, William L., and Vieth, Paul H. *Visual Aids in the Church.* Christian Education Press, Philadelphia and St. Louis, 1946, 214 pp., $2.00.

Sanderson, Dwight. *Leadership for Rural Life.* Association Press, New York, 1940, 127 pp., $1.25.

Slattery, Margaret. *A Primer for Teachers.* Harper & Brothers, New York, 1942, 141 pp., $1.50.

Smith, R. S. *New Trails for the Christian Teacher.* Westminster Press, Philadelphia, 1934, 260 pp., $1.50

Suter, John W. *Open Doors in Religious Education.* Richard Smith, New York, 1931, 128 pp., $1.25.

Vieth, Paul H. *How to Teach in the Church School.* Westminster Press, Philadelphia, 1935, 173 pp., $1.00.

————. *Teaching for Christian Living.* Bethany Press, St. Louis, 1929, 271 pp., $1.75.

INDEX